# Finish Well

Carolyn Flinn McCool

Acacia Publishing
Gilbert, Arizona

Copyright © 2011 by Carolyn Flinn McCool. All rights reserved.

No part of this publication may be reproduced, stored in a retrieval system or transmitted in any form or by any methods, photocopying, scanning, electronic or otherwise, except as permitted by notation in the volume or under Sections 107 or 108 of the 1976 United States Copyright Act, without the prior written permission of the author.

All quotes have been credited. Any omissions were not intentional. Quotes from Trail Markers are all anonymous. Derek Redmond's information was taken from the Internet, YouTube, and Wikipedia. All information was cited and can easily be found on the web or in print. Reminds me again, we stand on the shoulders of time and gracious people who have gone before us, teaching and telling.

Library of Congress Control Number: 2011912721

ISBN 978-1-935089-46-9

Cover Design by Jason Crye
Published by Acacia Publishing, Inc.
Gilbert, Arizona
ww.acaciapublishing.com
Printed and bound
in the United States of America

*Merk —*
*Finish what you started with Grace*
*Remember Vegas 2011,*
*Carolyn*

*Lovingly dedicated*
*Let's hear it for the boys — you are the best!*
*Thank you to all the men in my life…*
*For your fun, your laughter, your protection,*
*your different way of seeing things…*
*I have profited from you!*

*And to my sisters, all the girls in my life —*
*you really rock! I have always believed*
*I had the privilege of knowing the greatest people.*
*Thank you …*
*For your strong and available shoulders,*
*your wisdom that reaches deep,*
*and your love which is endless.*

*This book is dedicated to everyone*
*who taught me how to "dance."*
*I learned something from each of you,*
*even if there were times*
*I didn't wish for the lesson.*

# Contents

Acknowledgements
An Introduction and Purpose for Finish Well.......................... 1

## A RUNNER LOOKS AT THE RACE

Chapter One - Did He or Did He Not Finish Well? ............... 7
Chapter Two - The Friendship of Time ................................. 11
Chapter Three - Obstacles Might be Opportunities ............. 15
Chapter Four - People ........................................................ 19
Chapter Five - Events .......................................................... 23
Chapter Six - Illness and Injury ............................................ 25
Chapter Seven - Beliefs ....................................................... 29
Chapter Eight - When the Best of You Is Broken ................. 33
Chapter Nine - Forgiveness ................................................. 37

## PRE-RACE PACKET

Chapter Ten - Ask WHO ...................................................... 45
Chapter Eleven - Ask WHAT ................................................ 49
Chapter Twelve - Ask WHEN ................................................ 53
Chapter Thirteen - Ask WHERE ........................................... 55
Chapter Fourteen - Ask WHY ............................................... 57
Chapter Fifteen - Ask HOW .................................................. 59

## THE RUNNER'S COURSE

Chapter Sixteen - The Written and Learned-from Past ......... 65
Chapter Seventeen - The Opportunistic Present .................. 69
Chapter Eighteen - The Unwritten Offering Future ............... 73
Chapter Nineteen - Love vs. Fear ......................................... 77
Chapter Twenty - The Rhythm of Change and Transition .... 81
Chapter Twenty-one - The Opportunity For Men ................. 87
Chapter Twenty-two - The Opportunity For Women ........... 93

## TRAIL MARKERS

Marker 1 - True North, True You ......................................... 101
Marker 2 - Love Extravagantly ............................................. 105

Marker 3 - Finish Off Fear and Doubt ................................. 111
Marker 4 - Say It, Do It ........................................................ 115
Marker 5 - Caution Ahead ................................................. 119
Marker 6 - That's the Way It Is — or Is It? ............................ 123
Marker 7 - Confidence Grows Here .................................... 127
Marker 8 - Find Creativity and Contentment ....................... 131
Marker 9 - Affectionately Yours ........................................... 135
Marker 10 - Live Your Own Life ......................................... 139
Marker 11 - Express Gratitude for Wounds ........................ 143
Marker 12 - Find Your Voice ............................................... 147
Marker 13 - Remember and Reminisce .............................. 151
Marker 14 - Remember To Be Kind .................................... 155
Marker 15 - Be Ready to Live, Ready to Die ...................... 159
Marker 16 - Run With Wonder ............................................ 161
Marker 17 - Health and Wealth = Friends .......................... 163
Marker 18 - Train Your Thoughts, Trust Your Gut ............... 165
Marker 19 - Expert Advice Recommended ......................... 171
Marker 20 - My Success is Not Your Success ..................... 175
Marker 21 - Bad Day, or Is It? ............................................. 177
Marker 22 - Run Clean ....................................................... 181
Marker 23 - Make Love to Life ........................................... 185
Marker 24 - Marry Your Best Friend .................................... 189
Marker 25 - Don't Sell Anything .......................................... 195
Marker 26 - Details and Small Things, Please .................... 199
Marker 27 - Shoulder a Burden .......................................... 201
Marker 28 - Go Away .......................................................... 205
Marker 29 - Celebrate Moments ......................................... 209
Marker 30 - Race With All Ages ......................................... 213
Marker 31 - Time to BE First .............................................. 217
Marker 32 - Create a Legacy .............................................. 221

### AFTER THE RACE — A RUNNER'S REFLECTION

Experience It All...A Blessing From Your Senses ................ 227
Exit and Arrival .................................................................. 229
Ideas That Travel Well as You Finish Well .......................... 231
All I Have Learned ............................................................. 233
About the Cover ................................................................. 237

# Acknowledgements

No one, for the most part, gets anywhere alone. We "stand on the shoulders" of those before and beside us. What would we do without those "shoulders?" Yes, to some extent we run alone, but ultimately we run with others. Thank you to everyone whose shoulders I stand on and walk beside. I am deeply touched by those who have led me to believe, "She's not heavy, she's my sister."

My father always told me courage was doing what you must when you can't. Dad, you were my first cheerleader and courage-giver as you were always helping me on the course of life and getting me to the finish line. Even though I do not have you today, your words walk with me and guide me. Mom, no one has more strength than you. If I can be half the woman you are, I will be a tower of strength.

To the wonderful heritage and family I have, through all we have had, I love you so. From the sons who say, "Nerd, I love you," and "Mom, you're the best," to the people I work with who have been a part of resurrecting my life, I am indebted. To the one who rules the earth and who brings me the portion, both easy and hard, to create life from where "all blessings flow."

*Carolyn Flinn McCool 2011*

## An Introduction and Purpose for *Finish Well*

"All I Have Learned I Wanted to Share" was the beginning for *Finish Well*. It was a collection of thoughts, gathered far and wide, near and dear. I wrote it as a pamphlet and it has now become some of the ideas for *Finish Well*. You can find it on the last page of this book.

*Finish Well* is a look at some of the ingredients of a life that will finish well. It is not an exhaustive or mandatory list, as there are so any ingredients that conspire to create a life that finishes well. It is just a look at some of the common and uncommon trail markers on the road to finishing well. I wrote this book as I was getting some perspective after a difficult time. This difficult time, catapulted my life into such discouragement, where I didn't feel I could get back into life. My cry to someone was, "I just wanted to finish well."

Since getting up, I realize falling down does not disqualify you on the race to finish well; it qualifies you to re-enlist and reinvent! It screams at you to come back and be better, not in the reward and punishing way of "do it or else," but in the way that your past and experience will work good for you. This "good" works, even when you don't believe it or can't seem to find it! Time, a friend (I once did not like this friend), has ways of doing this.

This race of life and its challenges are not foreign to any of us. All challenges are not equal (I just thought mine was the hardest). Our challenges usually differ, if only in degree. Some face very large ones, where they bear up strongly, while other's challenges may seem easier, and they find it difficult to stand (assuming is dangerous). We both have one, of many things, in common; we want to live a productive and happy life...we want to finish well.

*Finish Well's* aim is to present an honest look, at real places we are in life and refuses to give a high thought without a humble look! Being so tired of "Superman Thinking" sites and books, this is neither! I so believe in positivity and mental assent, I just believe most people are struggling, growing, questioning, and learning in these areas throughout their whole lives in the process to finish well.

Talking about these places is a beautiful way to meet people at the heart level and fashion something good from our challenges. I write from being there and learning there. This learning and struggling is not a once-and-done deal! Every day you and I are asked to come to the plate and swing!

I wrote *Finish Well* for me because some of these "trail markers" were some of my instructors. I also wanted to give my children something tangible of the great intangibles in life. Lastly, I wrote for those who were precious to me. You know who you are. You know who I am, and that is good enough for me. I write also to offer encouragement for you on the road you are travelling

Your life counts. Your thoughts affect how you feel. How you feel affects how you act. How you act determines

*Introduction and Purpose*

how you will finish. Did you ever stop to realize how many people have been influenced by your life, positively or negatively? Everything counts, in ways you know and don't. That is not spoken to create pressure, but to free you to realize how valuable your life is!

*Finish Well* reads with 32 trail markers, one for every day of the month, with an extra for celebrations! Enjoying a book near you, at your beside or coffee table, brings you the company of finishing thoughts. This book is written with everything I've got and I want nothing less than to leave all of me here. As you travel life, I wish you "suitcases of hope" which will serve you well as you seek to FINISH WELL.

*Finish Well*

# A RUNNER LOOKS AT THE RACE

# Chapter One
# Did He or Did He Not Finish Well?

It was 1992, the Olympics in Barcelona, Spain. Derek Redmond, a United Kingdom sprinter, who held the world record, jumped out of the blocks on his way to a 400-meter semifinal qualifying heat. As the race neared the halfway mark, something went wrong. Derek pulled up; he could barely walk. The announcer spelled it out, "He has broken down."

What happened after this shocking event, that stunned the spectators, may be more amazing than a gold medal finish. Derek straightened up. He hobbled onward to the finish line. A man pushed through the crowds lining the track, and onto the racecourse, through security to Derek. With emotion the two men embraced and Derek leaned on the man, as he continued his "run" to the finish line. This man was Derek's father.

Derek finished the last 250 meters, injured, with his father at his side. When he and his father crossed the finish line, the stadium of 65,000 gave them a standing ovation.

His father, wearing a Nike "Just Do It" hat, said, "He had to finish, we started together."

Derek's tragedy and triumph is forever recorded on YouTube. His race is inspirational, his spirit unbreakable. What is more amazing to me, if that is possible, is what he did when the race was not going as planned. It is hard to "finish well" when the race takes you in a direction away from your dream. He could have quit, his dream dashed, but he went on.

After Barcelona, a surgeon told him his injury would never allow him to run again or compete for a country in a competitive sport. Derek went on to play basketball for a Great Britain team and rugby for his native land. He later sent the surgeon, who said he would never run or compete, a signed photo of his newfound success. Today, Derek serves as a motivational speaker. Derek Redmond finished well. The Olympic records mark Derek as a "DNF" (did not finish), but most people would not agree. He finished well in the greatest race, the race of life, that we run every day.

Everyone has a story like Derek's, though every story is different. Often, you don't get to pick your troubles, and all troubles are not equal. The race of life is a difficult one. If you do not believe that, you have not been in the race for very long or you are in a place of ease. Someone once said, "If you don't have any trouble now, get ready, you will someday." That someone was older and wiser, but I reasoned I was different because I would try harder.

I thought I could make my life easier with a few tweaks and tips, so I dismissed that notion. My promise was "if you trust God and do right, you will have a good and fairly trouble-free life." I had this attitude most of my adult life. I do not today. I have seen and experienced too much, that I have come to the conclusion "the race is hard but you can run to finish well."

## Can I welcome a crisis?

A crisis, large or small, gets you ready for something. It is a "gotta move on, up, or out" sign. For years I tried to avoid difficult or challenging places or gingerly step around them, now I want to use them instead of fear them! A crisis or difficult challenge has growth, compassion, love, and hope stamped all around it. It will make you better and it will make someone else better.

A crisis hands you the opportunity to see what you are made of, what you love, what you want, and what you place your hope is in. Knowing these things can be very helpful for you and they will answer some of your important questions about life. A crisis can make you live better and most importantly, the direction you take in or following a crisis can help you to finish well.

A crisis asks you to "give it time." It is like a signal for a "vacation from life as you know it!" Rather than fear a crisis, let it walk you through the places you need to visit. Let time be the friend that joins you. Though we may want to, try to never rush through a crisis, its lessons are life-altering opportunities to finish well.

Derek Redmond was determined to finish in spite of injury and reason. The stretchers came out, signaling the race was over, but his will said persevere. His crisis moved him "up and out," showing the world how to finish well. Run with me.

*Finish Well*

## Chapter Two
## The Friendship of Time

It's not how fast you go, but how well you cover ground. Remember the tortoise and the hare's race? Faster is not always a finisher. Life is like that, too. The stronger and the swifter do not always get the prize. The hare was clearly the quicker critter, but whoever wrote the story or proverb knew something we all need to know…it's how you run the race that will determine how you finish. Running the race with patience and time is a very good strategy.

What, even in trial, deep, deep trial? Yes. Difficult? Yes. Tearful? Yes. Impossible? No, though it feels like it sometimes! Comparing who has the worst troubles is not a worthwhile pursuit, though we may. Troubles are troubles, real and hurtful to the individual. You and I do not know someone's exact trouble, but compassion asks us to understand, even when we don't.

Time does not heal all wounds, but time does seem to soften them. We understand, through time, we forgive, through time, we hope, in time, we rise up after a fall, in time. Time often presents itself as a friend, while we may think it is an enemy. Look for time's friendship and you will have someone to walk through life.

Every day people are running the race of life and finishing well. From Derek Redmond to the ill woman I met at the grocery store to the aspiring and hopeful college student, these people want to finish well. Those who have fallen more on the racecourse seem to have more to give, in time. Choice wine comes from the crushed grape. Is this not part of the purpose of life and time...crushing for something beautiful to make and enjoy?

## Time, the friend you must have

Time can also feel like the racer's friend and enemy. Time represents a dual-edged sword. Time allows for recovery on the course to gather and go again. Time is best seen as a friend and it is good to walk friendly with time. Do we not get pleasure from watching children grow and develop a skill that only improves with the passing of time? Is it not right to celebrate an accomplishment that happens over the progression of time? The tortoise knew that time was his friend in the steady using of it; while the hare thought he had plenty of it and used it without proper pacing.

The enemy of time is thinking you have too much of it or not enough. When you think you have too much time, you can be aimless and lost in direction or purpose. When you think you have too little, your power transfers to fear and every action pulls you to finishing afraid.

The mystery is we do not know how much time we have, but we know we have time, today. Would we really

## The Friendship of Time

do better with time, if we knew we had a lot of it? Controlling the here-and-now and the what-we-have, bring you the opportunity to finish well by creating from what you have, not what you hope to have.

In a sense, time is controlled with patience. Have you ever seen the work of patience in someone's life? Quite a sight, indeed, is patience in love, work, and dreams. We often want an answer that is in tomorrow, today. That answer comes when time has fulfilled its obligations. You will know more about the best of life when you friend time and choose to walk side by side, instead of ahead. Just like "you can't hurry love," you can't hurry time.

Someone named Aesop knew the lesson and it is forever represented in this brief story of a tortoise and a hare, reminding us how to finish well…use the time, mind, and abilities you have to finish the race, to cover ground. The race is not always to the swift, but to those who faithfully race and patiently rise to finish well.

*Finish Well*

# Chapter Three
# Obstacles Might be Opportunities

In Phoenix, Arizona, there is a race with obstacles and plenty of mud called the Spartan Race. Competitors put their bodies and minds through agony and assault to cross the finish line to see what drives them, what is in them. The race of life has obstacles. Some will have more, some less. All will find them. It is man's lot in life; it is part of the journey.

I have to admit something here. I don't want them. I don't like them. I try to avoid them. I have found something strange about this idea of avoidance; you get your training from experiencing obstacles and entering in, not exiting out. Obstacles, like time, are your friends. You become more beautiful in mind and body with their persuasion. Obstacles are packaged for a real life, not an imaginary one.

Some obstacles will scratch you, others will bruise you, but some will open you up for a long time. All obstacles have the opportunity to give you something you will never get any other way…desire. Obstacles ask something of you like, "What do you want?" or "Where are you going?" or "What are you doing?" Good questions need good answers, supplied as you race to the finish line.

When I was younger, many things (buildings, objects, land areas) seemed so large to me. Even recently, my mother game me something I remember as being so large when I was a child, and to my surprise, it was really very small! I wonder…do we have things that we think are large in our lives (like obstacles) that are really small, or should be smaller than we imagine them to be?

## Obstacles come in all shapes and sizes

A size of an obstacle in a path does not always tell the degree of difficulty it will bring. Some obstacles that are small may derail one competitor, and a larger one may not. Some obstacles I write about are people, events, illness or injury, broken dreams, beliefs, and the issue of forgiveness. You usually cannot pick the obstacle and the size of it in your race. Sometimes you can jump over the obstacle, other times, the obstacle is an impasse in the race.

Once in a while, the obstacle will ask to travel with you. Sometimes, you will have to oblige. How you oblige will be your answer. A good friend who recently raced cancer and won said she learned, "What God takes you to, He will take you through." She was speaking of some challenging times she went through and this thought was her way to finish well.

Obstacles have hidden messages, similar to the enclosed message of a fortune cookie. They show you "what you are made of." In fact, they leave you with no doubt as to what you believe and what you are. Anyone can shine in prosperity; adversity reveals what you are deep, deep inside. This can be very scary, but it can be very comforting.

Some of the greatest movements in history came from obstacles. Look at the founding of America; do you see obstacles, nothing but obstacles? Many saw opportunities, nothing but opportunities! Nelson Mandela, Africa, prison, and pain birthed freedom. Obstacles redirect us and put us on roads we need to travel. When you think of rejection, remember Abraham Lincoln. "Failed" was written all over him on his political journey, while years later being elected President. Reading his "Emancipation Proclamation" speech shows he was made for "such a time as this."

This is our challenge, every day, to run with or through the obstacles along our course. As we age, we get many chances at doing a better job with the obstacles that come our way. Some of the obstacles are repeats, signaling to us we can learn more and be stronger. Some of the obstacles we believe will crush us are really our tickets to freedom and love.

Don't turn your back to the storms of life. As the wind blows to lift a jet upward, so troubles have their ways to lift you above them, and let you fly. What if you were to learn, someday, that your disappointments and difficulties were the stepping-stones to a richer and fuller life? Would you not, then, be even more thankful, and have more to give? Setting your face to the storms allows you to take that ride higher.

In the next chapters let's look at some of the obstacles that can be opportunities, as they are messengers bringing something to use for a meaningful life.

# Chapter Four
## People

If you are running the race, you are running it with people. Now that is good news and bad news. Good news is you have plenty of company. The bad news is, sometimes that company is not so pleasant.

This is life, yours and mine. People, we do need each other, but we can hurt each other. It wouldn't take you a minute to recall a past or present hurt. We all have them or will have them.

A broken heart or dream finds many of us at varying times in our lives. I have heard men wish they didn't let that girl get away or they would have taken that risk in a business deal. Women have told me they "settled" when they chose a mate, trying to please their parents and left their lover confused and lost after the breakup.

Some are in marriages where they are committed to doing the right thing but they have lost the spark of life on their race. The outside may look very good, but no one sees the inside that is swirling with loss and sadness.

In my high school yearbook someone signed it and closed with, "Remember, life is a do–it-yourself job." I agree, except living involves people and whether you live alone or not, they do factor in the enjoyment and experience of life. I will go as far to say that a "lone" life misses something, people only give. You cannot go alone.

An African proverb states, "If you want to go fast, go alone; if you want to go far, go together." This, to me, is absolutely true in the sense that you, alone, can do what you want to do and get somewhere, but you will go further on the road of life with others. Further is found in love, enjoyment, and opportunities.

## *Relationships bring the opportunity for pain and healing*

What about the obstacle of people? People hurt people from time to time. Even those you love can hurt you. Sometimes emotional wounds can hurt as much as physical ones. A recent USA Today article mentioned scientists have found heartbreak can show up by creating physical illness! The article stated the pain of the mind showed up as pain in the body. Experiences form impressions; we long carry into our walks of life and in our bodies.

How we are viewed and view people affects the challenge we have with being a part of the human race. A young girl learns early in life what many others prize, beauty and nice clothes on a good figure. Janice Ian with her song "At Seventeen" struck a chord with many women. The song addressed insecurities we have at young ages, especially for women considering beauty and worth. Both men and women ask the question, "Am I attractive and valuable?" Appearance plays a great deal in relationships, though we would like to think it not so. Once a friend, who was very beautiful, told me it was difficult being attractive because she never knew if someone liked her for her personality or looks.

Sometimes the hurt we have between people can be because we did the hurting. We can hurt people without intending to hurt them. Sometimes they will not forget or forgive. When you forever change a relationship, though you never intended or tried to purposely hurt someone, it hurts deeply. Sometimes a situation gets out of hand and the goodwill falters and the relationship dies.

Failing at a relationship of value is costly. You can feel very beaten down and this is no place anyone wants to fail. The truth is, we do fail with people, even if we really do not wish it so. This obstacle in the race can become your future trophy. The new skills you learn about accepting your mistakes and theirs can be your reward!

It takes time and love to get up and get going, living with a portion of resolve in an unresolved situation. This obstacle can become an opportunity, but it is hard to see it as such at the time. Being kind to you is where you accept and understand your limitations, wounds, and mistakes.

"Perfect is the enemy of the good," says a quote by Voltaire. Treasuring the good and leaving perfect unmeasured is a way to travel now. After sufficiently being disappointed with yourself for not achieving a certain standard, it serves everyone best to take and make something of what you have, not destroy everything because of what you do not.

People, even ourselves, can be a great obstacle in the race. They can slow you down, speed you up, and turn you out. Obstacles are really opportunities in disguise when your heart will not be shut to them and to people who make them. Still, people who need people are truly the luckiest people in the world. Thank you, Barbara Streisand.

# Chapter Five
# Events

Things happen. I think there is another phrase, but you get the picture. The flight attendant referred to it on a flight I recently took as "shift happens." She mentioned this to the passengers about how cargo can move around and it must be secured before takeoff. One day the race is easy and comfortable. The next, everything has shifted, sometimes forever.

The beautiful baby you have longed for is lost to miscarriage and people (who I am convinced only mean well) say, "It's for the best, something must have been wrong with the baby." Your husband is diagnosed with cancer or your wonderful father loses his life from a farm equipment accident. The stories could go on. You know them, too; they are all around you, maybe it is your story.

Events, happy and sad, shape you and your world. Like a rose with a beautiful bud on the end, so are thorns on a stem. Beauty and pain ride on the same stem of life. Someone mentioned to me, if you climb the thorns, you get to the bud, the beauty. I like that! Events shape us on

## Finish Well

the race precisely like that, when we let them.

Life's race will either make you bitter or better, I've heard it said. There is plenty to make either; the choice begins with us. How we choose and how we feel, will spell how we act, and the circle continues. Think well, feel better. Think bad, feel, well, worse. It is not merely mind over matter. You cannot will everything by determination or feelings, but you can take the obstacle of events and find some opportunities.

Happiness is not a constant walk in favorable circumstances. If that were so, there would be few happy people. Happiness comes from the way you travel in life, in the small and large things that touch you! There will be wonderful moments in our lives that come to us that create the feelings and joy of happiness, many of those moments, however, we must design and develop.

It is a wonder to see someone without a leg walk or without arms paint. Sometimes those with less, do more, perhaps, because they want to. Years ago I listened to a man with cerebral palsy speak, and in his slurry speech he said this about trying, "You have to have the want to." I never forgot his words and I challenge myself in running life's race by asking, "Do you have the want to?"

The race of life has no strangers when it comes to obstacles and challenges. Obstacles fit into our life's run for long or short stretches, but the obstacle of events can bring new views and opportunities when you run, desiring to finish well. Life is a hard ride; get a soft seat I once read.

# Chapter Six
# Illness and Injury

What would the world be like without illness or injury? Did you ever think of that? As much as it would be excellent, do you realize the gifts of these twins? Gifts such as compassion, patience, forgiveness, endurance, love, and aid to our fellow man might be lost. A news article on young children who lost family members to war, said their difficult experience had taught them to be more compassionate toward others. The one with the pain becomes more compassionate; maybe pain, which I do not like, has some purpose.

A man I know lost his health. After many months without a diagnosis, his world started to fall apart. Later he received a diagnosis and finds his condition to be managed, not cured, and perhaps never to be cured. This health obstacle created an opportunity for his lifelong desires. He quit his job and is pursuing his dream of helping others. Illness, an obstacle, gave him a new direction. Many will profit from his obstacle, even he will.

A young man's career pursuits are derailed by a shoulder injury. Uncertainty is introduced in his days, leading him to examine his life. His time off leads him to live somewhere where he meets his life long partner as he is sidelined by injury. This unwelcome event becomes a welcome to a new life. There are millions of stories like this; perhaps, you know one.

Illness is hard. In quiet places we ask a lot of questions of ourselves, others, and God. The obstacle of illness and injury asks us to come to terms with life…and sometimes death. Being afraid of the questions only keeps the answers far away. It is safe, we can ask and we can patiently seek some answers. It is okay to live the unanswered questions but it is never okay to believe the obstacle of illness and injury have no purpose or direction for our lives or others.

## A young soul with an old lesson

Mattie was my hero. He left this world at 13. His *USA Today* memorial still rests in my address book, where I can find his smiling face and remembrances (I even sent his mother a sympathy card, though I never met her). He was born with a crippling disorder, but he was one of the most alive and "straightened" souls I know. His books identified him in this manner: "Written and illustrated by Mattie J.T. Stepanek, poet and peacemaker. Mattie fought his terrible illness, but he won, and so did those who walked along with him.

Never do I want to leave you with the impression that illness and injury is a place of celebration and everything rolls smoothly and works out well. That would be the farthest thing from the truth. Every person I have shared with you had hard dealings with places of illness or loss. Every loss stings and echoes at different times and in unusual places. A lot of tears were cried and were never wasted.

Some stories do not have these types of "happy" endings; I have seen those, too. What I also have seen, in most every story, is something reaches someone or the one, who is ill, and they are never the same, or they are challenged by the event. What is memorable and important to share is that with time as your friend, patience, and hope in God (and all three can seem far at times), what is loss, what is an obstacle, can lead you to a place on the course of life to finish well.

Quitting is an option. Suicide is, too, but what do they solve or resolve? I do not say that lightly, either. I have been places that make me look at others and life very differently now. Suicide ends one pain and creates a hundred. I have a mathematician's mind and those stats don't look too good. I understand both kinds of pain in new ways.

When an obstacle is very large, hope is lost or at least deferred. The heart finds itself in a difficult place. A runner who travels with hope will carry the obstacle differently than one without hope. Hope stems from our belief systems that I will cover in the next chapter.

*Finish Well*

# Chapter Seven
# Beliefs

It is a given, we all believe something about life's views and race of life. Every person alive has a belief system stemming from many people, places, and senses. I am no expert with a PhD on this subject, but no one graduates from the school of continual learning, a place we learn very much. I share from much reading and reviewing of life, but no formal stamp of approval! I enjoy the sharing of differing opinions on the matter, leaving myself sharpened and open, but with growing and changing convictions.

A proverb in the Bible states, "As a man thinketh, so he is." Many other religions and cultures have similar thoughts. This "thinking" factors into who we are and our enjoyment of life. When I was younger I would hear the phrase, "a mind is a terrible thing to waste" in an advertisement on television. How true, how absolutely true. The mind's power and use cannot be overstated, our mind in a sense, creates reality and brings productivity.

Whatever you believe about someone, something, or yourself forms your world. I will not write about the case for God, that has been done, beautifully, just look outside. It has always been harder for me to not believe God exists than He does; believing He doesn't seems to take greater faith. How I fit in this world stems from what I believe about this world. I do not know a lot of things for sure, as I am sure you would confess; life does contain mystery.

What you and I believe about life, will affect how we do life! If I have crushing views of God as punisher and judge, it will affect how I make my decisions and see my errors. If I believe I am loved without condition, I will live in that mind set, be free to love, and embrace life. Others will be touched by what you and I believe; beliefs are far reaching, they touch more people than we will ever be able to count.

I know a man who always felt God was against him because he could rarely complete a round of golf without a major disaster on some hole (golf is not easy to play, my non-golfing readers). He was a very good player and would play well as things went along smoothly, then something, not according to plan would show up, and he would explode, or should I say implode. He would berate himself and scream. It was agony to watch his decline and emotions, even harder to watch his fall later in life. I have been here, only to a lesser degree, I do not say this to judge him, and I am no great example and I have parts of my life where I do not think right.

## Shattered beliefs

You probably know where I stand in many ways with a belief system, but I respect and will listen to yours. I want you to know that I have struggled with the God I believe in. Struggled with what I know, what I read and what I have experienced. I prayed before I wrote this, that doesn't make it inspired, but I hope it leads you to understand this subject has deeply touched my race and me.

When my world shattered, I lost, or so I thought, everything I believed in. Everything that hit me was tested with my belief system and no sense or understanding enlightened me. It was very dark and I saw the ceiling way more than I wish anyone would. I learned one thing, however, what I believe follows how I will live.

Those who loved me carried my burden a few steps with me and some, many steps. Those who loved me let me know they loved me. When someone won't give up on you, it sure helps you not want to give up on yourself. I needed someone to be there and needed to see God like that.

One of my friends challenged me to "flip the coin" when I had a belief about a person or a matter, as there are more then one-way to see things. This practice helped me see the other side of beliefs and views. It has actually helped me look to understand, and not merely want to be understood. Sometimes, I have learned, people hurt people because they are hurting and afraid. Fear is a bad motivator, but so many, like me, was motivated from fear rather than love when I was at my lowest.

Having hope is part of belief. It has been said one can live without water for a few days, food for several days, but never can one live without hope. Hope is a great asset and friend on the road to finishing well. A belief will create an action, within and without. What you believe shows up in everything you see, say, do, and touch. Beliefs are strong obstacles…but even stronger opportunities on the road of life. Proper discipline and perseverance in belief will hold you up when obstacles threaten to pull you down.

# Chapter Eight
# When the Best of You Is Broken

I don't like when I break something, especially something that was valuable or sentimental to me. What is more difficult is when something breaks inside of you because of something valuable or sentimental to you. Broken dreams are like that, they may happen outside of you, but they deal the toughest blow inside of you.

Every one is touched by broken dreams. Some people seem to find their dream and live it while others hunt, fight, and still it eludes them. The importance of the dream will determine the gravity of the fall. The more you wanted it, the more it will be painful without it. It can seem and be very dark at some times in our lives with the broken wing of a dream.

So how does one get up after being so down? No formula again. I so wish I had a formula, sometimes, it would make it so much easier, but life gives us a little light and asks us to keep a lot of hope.

It may be easy to tell someone that all things work for good or it will be what it will be. When you do that without listening to the depths of someone's heart, the pain is just a little deeper. One of the greatest friends of life is the friend of compassion. Compassion is just saying, "I'm going to stay a little longer with you and understand a little more."

Broken dreams are not quickly fixed like broken items. The repair work usually takes much longer and is more costly. Things can end very badly for broken dreams. The opportunity of new dreams can rise from brokenness. You may not believe that or want that at the time, but if you can keep walking and keep your heart open, you might find the chance for beautiful dreams again.

One of the reasons we love comeback stories is because of someone finding something they lost or capturing something they should have had. The Olympics play this out every season. The stories and the athletes get into our hearts and our lives. Their stories are brought to us and they resonate with us. We love watching someone overcome (as well as we like the giant to be toppled sometimes). Maybe because this is our story to some degree, some time.

Comeback stories give us hope that we, too, might find that place in our lives. When something in us is broken, if we travel with hope that dreams, if even in a different form or kind may come back to us, we can find encouragement. That story you just saw on TV might be your story tomorrow. Losing hope and losing opportunities can break a life, a family, and a future. You may never know how a day may change, both for good or bad.

Staying in the race when you get bad news or an opportunity passes you by is very difficult. We get this in aging. I will never get the chance to be Miss America (not that I want to, but I am showing an opportunity passes at points in our life), I have passed the age deadline. I will never be able to do some things again, that time has passed. That is hard when an era goes by. It is hard when you have run the race and not been present to life around you and time seems up. Middle age has a way of doing that to you. There is lots of talk about that, but until you have been there, you can never appreciate the place.

A broken dream can leave you with some wishes unfulfilled. Those are other obstacles in the race of life. Part of how we live is dependent on how we think we will live tomorrow. If you travel and believe hope is always knocking at the door, you can be assured it will come in. It is not merely that hope did, it is partly because you wished to perceive it this way. Wishful thinking, it is not, wishing and doing seem to find people finishing well.

Every disappointment in our lives has another message written on it. We may not be able to uncover it today, but it does have something to say to us about our life. Holding on when our grasp is weak is where our will and beliefs keep us in the game. Having wonderful friends and family when you just can't hold on will help you do what you so desperately need.

That lost championship, that failed spot to be placed on the team, or that partner you really wished for have gone. Their place is not going to be replaced by the same event or person, but the replacing just might find you stronger, wiser, and more hopeful. The place where broken dreams dump you just might be a place of more dreaming and more fulfilling than you might once have imagined.

That place only comes to those who risk it all, to quest to find what they so deeply desire.

# Chapter Nine
# Forgiveness

No writing about the race of life would be complete without the subject of forgiveness. Forgiveness cements the best of life to your heart and soul, to your journey, today, here on earth. If you know and have experienced forgiveness, your life and heart are more full and whole. If forgiveness has eluded you, the opportunity begins now. If not from another extending it to you or you to them, maybe you will extend forgiveness to you, for something you are holding onto.

Last summer I witnessed a miracle. Well, at least to me it was. A woman who was intoxicated had plowed into a van killing a woman's daughter. How much hate do you think could be generated from this action to a grieving mother and family? Can we say, "A whole lot?" What was remarkable as I watched this video of two women was the remorse of the lady who drove drunk in accepting her crime, but what astonished me was the mother of the lost child!

She was open, frank, and honest. I like that. That is the best way to run the race in finishing well. You cannot solve a problem from dishonesty. Yes, it is hard to "face the music" but honesty is where healing begins. Honesty brings peace to the body and mind.

The woman proceeded to talk about the accident and the pain, but she continued by saying she and this woman have become good friends and she forgives her (the woman causing the accident has been disciplined by law, serving time)! Wow, I have not been in her shoes, but I do not know if I could do what she has done. I would want to, but a child, a loss, forever! I would want to hate, at least a little while longer, I am afraid to admit.

Every day I see little miracles in the lives of ordinary and extraordinary people. If I stopped travelling the road of forgiveness I would shut this out of my life (and forgiveness is often a hard road to travel). Forgiveness exposes our own heart, as well as the one in the story with us. The world can feel barren and numb without a forgiving and giving heart.

## The choice you can't refuse

Forgiveness is a choice you and I make every day, it is not a once and done deal, like it was once portrayed to me. You and I will struggle with forgiving, so our decision to forgive must come from the place where we are…NOW! You can't think of yesterday's forgiveness (I did it already) or hope for tomorrow's (I will do it later), you can only choose to give the "gesture of tomorrow" today (forgiveness opens tomorrows for you and the other person). Choosing activates with the grace given and needed to allow you and others a walk close to the divine, the supreme place of love. Forgiving a lover, a friend, or an enemy is an action of the highest good you can do or give. The ripples and sprinkles from forgiveness, or the lack of it, long leave their marks, on people and generations to come.

Offenses come up between people every day, people close to you and others you must deal with in life who rub your world. Some offenses are greater and others, more frequent. You get an assignment every day when your feet hit the floor. Will you be kind? Will you be forgiving? So much is riding on your choice — the choice to forgive.

Someone really hurt you or you hurt him or her; I am walking in your shoes, too. I can feel hate and hurt and so can they, but what will that accomplish for me, for them, for you? Your apology may have not been accepted; that cuts deeply. It is a little death to not be able to mend what is broken. We do what we can, not what we can't; love must be trusted to find a way and cover the rest. This is a place to grow not to be torn down forever.

## The heart of forgiveness

While forgiveness is a desirable and life — giving choice, it doesn't merely mean one weighs the obstacles and opportunities, as one does with other choices. Being stingy and evaluative should never rest near the place of forgiveness. The good and the better onto the finish line are through the paths of forgiveness. Forgiveness is never a bad road choice, for anyone. This is where the struggle comes in after the choice to forgive — how will life look? — things are now changed.

Sometimes it just takes time for both, you and the person, to work through the process of forgiveness. Some relationships go forward easily after forgiveness has been given. Though the concept can be accomplished immediately, the work of forgiveness is ongoing because we are very human. Forgiving is a delicate work, growing best when handled gently and served with time. Give the hours and days the space to work on the change you are working toward. You cannot drag someone along to the place you want to meet with him or her in the forgiveness equation. You will damage any goodwill if you do this.

Emotions open us up very deeply in situations where guilt and anger played a part. We don't know how to handle that much emotion at times. You know your side and they know theirs; it hurts to not have a bridge over the pain that joins you. Each person has time for work to go on in their souls while they are apart. We can have a measure of peace when we are pulling for each heart to grow during this awkward time of conflict. This is a great time to learn to wish the offended or offender well. Wow, what it will do to your thought life! Many people see the day where forgiveness does come — that is some beautiful day!

There will always be situations where forgiveness seems outrageous to give or receive. Those are the places and people where forgiveness is all the more needed. You may let someone find a way to return to life when you forgive. You may even rescue your own life when you forgive someone for the pain they brought you. Show me one person who lived better through hatred and conflict with another rather than the gift of forgiveness and restoration. Forgiveness gives a heart a new look and work. Never easy, often difficult, but always something good is birthed from forgiveness.

Have you learned this lesson? When forgiveness is practiced and practiced often, you will have friends and family on the race with you. The action of forgiveness has healed more hearts and calmed more spirits than all medical procedures or medications. Its application involves risk and humility, two gifts that scare most of us, but two gifts that work magic. Run with forgiveness.

*Finish Well*

PRE-RACE PACKET

# Chapter Ten
# Ask WHO

A journalist subjects himself to observation. He gathers information and then scatters it, with the anticipation it brings more to his readers. WHO is one of the first questions for him and WHO is a good question on the journey to finish well.

The world is filled with people, some you will never met and some you will, and some you wish you didn't. People make life better or worse. Asking WHO you are and WHO you will run this race with are fundamental and necessary reflections in life.

Do you know WHO you are? I am still in this school-that-never-ends and I can safely say, you probably still are. Have you had the privilege of recognizing the deep gifts you have, the unique offerings only you can bring to your existence, and the sides of you, both glorious and awful, you wish even you didn't know at times?

The gift of time will bring you this WHO you are person and it is a beautiful one! Talking about WHO you are, again, asks and answers a lot of questions and offers a lot of peace. Better to shake hands with WHO you are now, than break company with WHO forever.

It is easy to both simultaneously love and hate WHO you are. Well, maybe not at the exact moment, but perhaps, in the same day. Finding WHO you are and taking him or her home makes for great dinner conversation, as well as any time conversation. WHO you are is a product of so many places multiplied by all your experiences and thoughts. WHO you are is just amazing. I hope you know WHO and take care of WHO!

WHO you find yourself in life with is way, way important (this note is for you my sweet boys, especially). WHO you dance with will either wear you out or invigorate your life. WHO you "chill" with will make your life thrilling or have the potential to feel like they are killing you. You are on your own, but you do life with the WHOs in this world.

Some WHOs you cannot chose, they will just be there. It may even be the parents or parent you have, WHO you just don't like very much or the neighbor next door. You cannot run all the WHOs in your life out, but you can know WHO you are and have some say in WHO you travel with in the race.

WHO you walk with may lift you up or pull you down. A man hangs around with the wrong crowd. Many nights he is out with them while they stop at the convenience store. He waits in the back of the parked car. One night he is doing something different, so he is not with them. His peers get arrested that night. He finds out they have made it their fun to rob markets. He was along for the ride other nights, while they did this same thing unknowingly with him, but this night took him away. He was with the wrong crowd, and he didn't even know it! He goes on in life to have an important job in his work. That was a real story from my teenage years and I still have not forgotten it!

You can love the WHOs in your life that you find difficult to like, but when it is time, keep the WHOs you most trust to love you and be there, those very close to you. You may have a lot of acquaintances and Facebook friends may be numerous, but know the real count. Strive to impress and live contentedly with those you touch and who touch you in life. Those real WHOs will come in handy in seasons of doubt, difficulty, and disaster. I once read that friends are a good cushion in old age, I believe it.

WHO is truly a friend or a lover is needed information to finish well. It may be one or a handful, but you will do well to know who is in your camp...no matter what. Numbers do not count with WHO, no one can spread themselves that thin. Securing good relationships makes the wheels roll smoother on the journey to finish well. WHO will walk with you in life?

*Finish Well*

# Chapter Eleven
# Ask WHAT

Have you asked WHAT is important to you? Have you listened and made choices around that desire? In our youth we often don't fully know WHAT is important to us and sometimes it just takes years of living to see WHAT you can't live without or wish you could do. Be on the lookout for WHAT you wish to enjoy in your life. Being honest with your desires, even the not so "good" ones, will help you see WHAT you believe about you and life.

If you love family gatherings, it is probably not wise to move a 1,000 miles away from family for extended periods of time. If you want to see your grand kids, you might want to consider moving closer to see them, if that is very important to you and them.

Everyday life asks you to make choices and some of those choices need to be made in spite of the odds or difficulty because those choices are WHAT are important to you and WHAT you desire in life. The longer I live the more I realize, you and I have more power to create our lives then we can imagine.

When you have suffered a great blow, it is hard to pick up and go on, at least initially, for many of us. Sometimes the repair work takes even longer for others. The situation stands and will not presently change, so another WHAT thought is helpful. WHAT ARE YOU GOING TO DO ABOUT IT?

## WHAT to do

You cannot solve a problem from the point of the imaginary; problems are solved from the place of what is real — reality. Asking "What are you going to do about it?" puts you on freedom's ground to solve a problem from strength instead of weakness, reality, not illusion. Real problems have better opportunities to be solved over wishful ones. Wishing our problems away often leads us away from the solutions and closer to inaction. Inaction leads to no forward movement. We serve best in life when we honor ourselves in honest discussion about what is important to us. You cannot give from the best of you if you haven't respected your own needs.

I believe in self-interest. I believe God has never opposed it in its correct sense. The greatest scriptural commandment calls man to love God ... and your neighbor as yourself. I cannot know God's full intent, but proper care and value must find you to find others on the road to finishing well. The cup of life always pours out what fills it.

# WHAT price

Assigning proper value to your life is very essential to the question beginning with WHAT. The "pricetags" of life must be on the proper product. Materialism steals simple and great gifts in life. It creates confusion over value. I am not against "things;" I like "things." What is not good is when things become your and my identity or we become valuable for having them. I am more than my house or car, though I have both. WHAT you want to do and WHAT is important to you can get clouded with WHAT you have. They can shift your true compass, often very subtly. Awareness is the first defense and honesty a close second against living an unlived "well" life.

It is helpful to live your life with answered WHATs. Life gets busy, complicated, and cluttered. Asking these questions sooner rather than later helps direct you to finishing well. If you don't pay attention to your heart and WHAT you want, it will be easy to drift on down the road. Sometimes, you will live someone else's life if you drift and sleep. So many things vie for your time and heart, and then life is over. When you stand up to the plate and are ready to take the pitch, you can make something of your life!

*Finish Well*

# Chapter Twelve
# Ask WHEN

The Scripture teaches, "To everything is a season." Life teaches that lesson very well. What you can do at 16, you may not be able to do at 60. Babies can't drive motor vehicles at two and most teens cannot be self-supporting homeowners and family providers. In time, so much comes and goes. Time, life is made of time and seasons. WHEN to make choices or do things is the critical component of our lives and the quality of them.

Knowing WHEN is one of life's great challenges. WHEN may save you a lot of heartbreak. WHEN may keep you in life longer. Maybe it is just not time to have a baby at 13, even though you love kids and that cute guy. Maybe that sports car is not suppose to be in your driveway when you can't even pay the house payment.

WHEN is not lived by a formula. How I wished at times there was one in dating and career choosing, but life is not like that. It is probably best that it is like that because we would all be emotionally poor without some of the lessons life gives us.

Living and understanding WHEN will help you with timing and changes. In fact, anytime you are in a place of change, asking WHEN is a good question. WHEN is as important as the other "W's" and "H" questions. Getting WHEN right can be very satisfying and peaceful.

On the flip side, nothing ventured, nothing gained. If you are afraid to try or decide, will you ask WHY, so you will know WHEN? You will never make a directional change if you don't know or are afraid of WHEN is the time! Watch for being impulsive, but watch for WHEN. Impulse fears waiting, while WHEN is not hurried, but determined and committed to finding a good decision.

Taking a backseat and hoping you get a good ride is not truly participating in life. You cannot control all the choices or events in life, nor should you, but being involved in those things and people that matter to you can be spelled out in WHEN.

Answering WHEN helps you travel the road to finish well.

# Chapter Thirteen
# Ask WHERE

WHERE do you find comfort, direction, and peace? Many will say, God. An UPward look, both in the heart and head, sets for many, a life in motion or at rest. Others will answer in another fashion. I love the Psalm that offers, "I will lift up mine eyes unto the hills, from whence cometh my help." Sometimes God has not been my comfort and looking UP has been painful, but I find, through it all, that is the place I look again.

Looking OUT is another WHERE place. The world is so big and beautiful, even amidst such pain sprinkled throughout. I have to remind myself of that, often. There is the HOW coming in, needing to think well.

Looking OUT at your world and being there is WHERE we find so much of life. There is a job to do and you are needed. There are lives to reach and your hand is the one they want to hold! Don't let anything or anyone keep you from giving and loving your world, given to you to bless. This is WHERE you are supposed to be, looking OUT!

Looking IN finds you at rest and in conversation, as with a good friend. "Don't inspect your navel," as someone once told me, but do take the time to look here, IN. Sometimes life gets so busy, you may not even know you. Getting to know you is an interesting ride, a ride of appreciation and value. Finding your strengths and knowing your weaknesses build great confidence for living. Knowing WHERE to look — and from time to time, that is INward.

WHERE is a good look in many places. Your life will be richer for asking WHERE you find your strength, WHERE the world is you are called to serve, and WHERE you walk with the person you will walk the longest and furthest with — YOU!

# Chapter Fourteen
# Ask WHY

The significance of WHY cannot be overstated. WHY is asked very early in our lives as children in the quest to understand and WHY is an ever-present helper on the race to finish well.

WHY am I living life the way I am? WHY do I believe this? WHY am I doing this? WHY did I make that choice? WHY? I am sure you have asked these questions, both with someone and privately. WHY is one of the scariest and important words in the dictionary, both in the book and in your personal vocabulary. WHY always asks something of us. I have had to ask back, "Am I willing to listen and take an honest look at WHY?

WHY hurts. If often reveals your deepest feelings about something or someone. It makes what has been done, not be able to go away. It makes what might be, a certain direction I wish to travel.

WHY heals. It lets honesty in and refreshment come out. WHY may not solve all your problems, and it often awakens them, but it most definitely opens your understanding to living out the WHY of life with intention and purpose. It is no longer the "Accidental Life." WHY you are doing WHAT you are doing in your life, will help you with the answers to HOW to finish well. It is really that simple, it is just the doing that is so hard!

# Chapter Fifteen
# Ask HOW

HOW will you choose to live your life? You get the pleasure of living with you for all your life. HOW you will live your life will be determined by the way you think. What is important to you, you will move toward. It will begin with your thoughts, your thinking. HOW you think will affect everything you will do and experience. Take it further; it will affect everyone around you. That's a lot to bear, but it is true.

Never underestimate your thought life; it becomes your DO life. What you are doing right now is because of what you think, have thought, and if you keep thinking the same, will think and do. HOW you perceive things, HOW you learn things, HOW you approach life will be reflected at the thought level. HOW you feel is a signal to go back to WHAT you are thinking. If you feel bad, (unless you are sick or have a difficult experience you are going through) there is a possibility you might be thinking poorly.

Did that make your head spin? Thinking usually does. I have found one great gift in thinking. Thinking lends to an intentional life. Living intentionally means living on purpose. For the things dearest to me, I want to be intentional. Not that I do not care about small things (read about them in "Details and small things, please), but one only has so much energy. You are intentional without even noticing. You go to work, because you intend to do your job and you intend to get a paycheck, and you intend this to be the means to living your life. You get up, have your routine, get a cup of coffee, and do what you intend is next.

After the routine and what you have to do, have you asked if this is HOW you want to live your life? If not, look for ways to find HOW you want to live to make it happen on purpose. Your thinking is like the driving of a car, it will take you where you choose to go, you are steering. You may not get to miss the potholes from time to time, the narrow roads, or the stormy days, but you can show up by being in the driver's seat with HOW you will think.

Changing HOW you think begins with AWARENESS. Want to know what you are thinking? It will show you where you are heading. Write down what is on your mind every few hours and ask yourself how you feel (be way honest here). Try this for a couple of days, or a week, if you can keep up. You will learn a whole lot about yourself, some things you did not even realize. Look for the correlation between what you think and HOW you feel and what you then, do. It's an easy look where you take yourself every day and where you have habits.

Thoughts form habits and you know habits, good or bad, are hard to break. Asking HOW you think and feel are key reminders of HOW life is going with you and HOW you are spending it. Thinking well is an asset on the road to finish well and will be looked at a little later in "Train Your Thoughts, Trust Your Gut."

*Finish Well*

# THE RUNNER'S COURSE

## Chapter Sixteen
## The Written and Learned-from Past

When you are young, your past is virtually non-existent or small. In fact, someone younger reading this book may wonder and find it difficult to relate to the past being an obstacle. Youth from good homes and communities have past memories of happiness and accomplishment. Talk to someone older and wiser, and worn, and the past will have marks on him or her. Marks that show they were touched and weathered by the past, as well as marks that tell they have survived and thrived.

Just what is the past? Is it fair to say the past is anything behind you? Is it correct to say the past is affected by the present because the moments of today become the past of tomorrow very quickly? So would it be fair to say the making of the past is exercised in the present?

If yes is an answer to any or all of the questions above, then it is important to see the past is a period of time we have a present interest in. It is often spoken, "That's the past" and we understand that means it happened and is done. The always present contributes to our eventual past and forges us into our future. We affect the finish line by how we live today. The finish line is seen as a future stop, but in a sense, it is set before us in the present actions and duties we perform now!

Forgetting the past is like trying to not remember your name. It just won't happen. The past is woven in the fabric of who you are. Those fabric strings are placed to strengthen and add beauty to the canvas of your life. The past, joys, and sorrows, peace and turmoil, is designed to reflect the greater good your life brings, just like a beautiful garment you see in whole and not in part.

The past becomes an obstacle when you can't forget it while in the present pursuits of life. If our past cripples or lames us today, it has become a formidable obstacle. Every runner has some pull from the past. Some experience broken dreams, make mistakes, or failure shows up on the runner's journey. Sometimes the blame or cause is easy to place. We may have done something or someone may have. More still, sometimes both, they and we have contributed to a scar-making obstacle of the past. Are we done with the present and the future?

A runner set on finishing well, sets his eyes on the prize and can get up." A righteous man may fall seven times, but he gets up," the Scripture teaches. Did you get that — a righteous man even falls, but he gets up? The best or the better has thwarted plans and obstacles. We are in good company; we all fall. It is the act of getting up we must be engaged in.

*The Written and Learned-from Past*

Past sins haunt many, even though I read God has absolutely assigned them a place where he "remembers them no more." What if we lived and believed in full freedom from our errors? Would the finish line be worth pursuing heartily and with hope?

Past losses cost many the fear of going ahead. Some fear they are dealt with heavily because of them. Why? Are they? Those are unanswered questions, though people speak as if to know the answer for another one's fall. Leaving those unanswered questions cradled in mercy and hope will help everyone run to finish well.

You cannot write your future, you can only follow after it. The past has written its messages where the present can recall them, best done with love. Many past happenings were beyond your or my control and remain a mystery. Those we could control, maybe we did not control well. Was there something to learn? Is your heart longing to finish well? Let the past be where it must stay, though it is always a part of you, and let your present lend a voice of hope to finish well.

*Finish Well*

# Chapter Seventeen
# The Opportunistic Present

The present is much talked about these days and writers and teachers talk about "being in the present moment" to experience joy and life. The present is what you actually hold and have. It is the moldable material of dreams and desires, both now and tomorrow. The present, however, can be a stumbling block and obstacle, when you are not engaged in it. It can also be filled with fresh fire and opportunity.

Sounds very simple, but we may waste the present or remain disconnected to it. No one can be "on" all the time, but hopefully we will plug in to the present. The present is sometimes viewed as too wide and large to many, when it is really very specific and narrow. It, too, like the past or future has a place and that place is the moment, and moments do not wait. It is the moment you are breathing in, NOW!

Being awake to the present is the only way to experience it. The runner in the race does this best when he is rested, fed, and exercised to take on his tasks. He sees the needed preparation and is clued in to what needs to be accomplished or enjoyed. The present will not be an obstacle when opportunities and possibilities become an interest to living life.

When the journey to finish appears long, the more you profit from being in the present. When you savor the walk, the present can only be enjoyed. Being "brain dead" along the way from time to time may help you get along, but to finish well, you must be present participating.

I remember as a young girl, in Germany (many know I had the pleasure of going to high school there), waiting for the Homecoming Dance to come. I had the young man of my wishes, a beautiful dress, and something out of this world to wait for. I longed for that date. I love anticipation.

Anticipation is not over rated, but the present I left a little bit undone. I realized, as I got older, those days often do come. In fact, they come a lot sooner than I ever imagined. Yes, I should plan, prepare and be so excited, but I learned that celebrating today is the best defense to disappointment and expectation.

Many quotes reveal the need to enjoy the moment. Truly, the present is all we have, but in honesty we hope the future to come. Most of us find the future does come. It serves everyone best when we take the gift of the moments and throw them a party. Just for this moment I stopped to smile, to feel the cool breeze, and look at my resting cat on the sofa. Moments of awareness are sweet. This is what being present is all about, finding celebration in moments.

Too much doing and not enough savoring ruin the present. It is good to have a mission or calling, something to wake up to and for every day. Still, one may fail to experience the present when doing becomes one's only occupation, even doing that is well-doing. Peace with others and yourself is best enjoyed in the present. A peace that allows you rest in doing or resting is enjoying the opportunity of the present and finishing well. The present is yours, now.

Have you been hurried today? Yesterday? When we are in the middle of winter and it is bitter cold, we long for summer's warmth — and it comes. Nature never hurries its calendar. Seasons precisely and in their own time come to bring their differing delights and necessary objectives, unaided by us. Is this not wisdom for us today? Why do we really have to hurry? Is there not enough for us in the gracious use of the now? Enjoy the season you find yourself in, until time brings you another.

*Finish Well*

# Chapter Eighteen
# The Unwritten Offering Future

I love the thought of the future because it fills my seeking dreams. Somehow I get the idea I can do whatever I want in the future and I like that (I know this is not so). It challenges me in the present because I now understand how past, present, and future play in my life. Though I only "have" the present, the past shaped me and is the accumulation of all my "presents" and now, the future is made with my present conscious choices.

I create the future by creating it today. I know I do not control all the aspects of the future. It would be no fun to have no surprises! It would be horrible to know some of the troubles we or those we love may experience someday. Knowing what might happen can weigh down the present. Yes, sometimes, I would love to have my hand in the mix, but I humbly admit, I am challenged with my own life. I cannot run the world, as I so often have tried.

## The theme of the future

Hope is a greatest asset for the future. A child is a picture of hope to me, a life to come. A child brings newness and hope to life. Children remind me there is a tomorrow, even today. When I see a pregnant woman, I am reminded of hope to come. I once ran the race, for a time, without hope, because I felt no future. That is not a good feeling. In fact, no present can be enjoyed when you feel hopeless; no future comes into view either. Even people with terminal illnesses or pain often travel with hope, though the road can be dark, lonely, and difficult.

The finish line is a certain future event in everyone's life. Every one bats a thousand here. How well we see the obstacles and believe they can become opportunities will challenge us on our race. When you believe in the future, you can really live your life. When you believe in hope, you have a future without fear. A future with hope has many possible looks. It creates programs for the needy, gives food to the hungry, and rescues the sick and suffering, and everything more. The future looks bright with hope, dim without it.

The future always offers you an opportunity for hope. It is an unwritten tablet in a sense to us and we get to write on it. It is also like the story of the woven tapestry. We see the loose strings and raw product from the underside, but if you turn it to the other side, something beautiful appears. It is an exquisite finished product. It is the same item with the same threads, but how you turn it determines how it looks. This is the tapestry of our lives. We see them so up close and personal that we loose focus sometimes of the whole. Parents do this with children when they are exasperated from training or parenting and lovers do this with relationships when the best of each other is left out of focus. We are weaving something beautiful out of our lives that the future often gets the pleasure of seeing. How we must try to not lose heart when things are not going so well. If we can contribute to the present with what we can do, there will be something created for the future. This may at times seem not true, but you must keep travelling, you must not give up or in.

Hope seems to be in low supply in our world today, some would say. If I looked at the race of life from the world's troubles and this view only, I could agree. From the economy to just living the challenges of life, it is easy to feel this way. We were made to hope and long. Learning to "flip the coin" and hope gives another view and here I shall camp. Hope travels well on the way to finishing well. Read more about hope in "Bad day coming…or is it?"

*Finish Well*

# Chapter Nineteen
# Love vs. Fear

Love vs. fear. It sounds like a boxing match. Well, it is. It is the fight of life we find ourselves in every day. You and I make a choice to fight life on one side or the other. At the basic core of us, all of our choices stem from here. Fear is the universal paralyzer and dream killer. You won't even get out of the blocks if you answer to fear. Love releases the best in you and others. You may be alive, but you can't know life if you don't love.

I see the titles in print and I have heard them in speeches summing up how we negotiate life, responding either from love or fear. I like simple. Simple is easy and gets things done. If I could put life in a nutshell, I would use these two words, carried with this one thought. Life is lived in the place of love or fear, every day and in every way it comes to you. How will you define these words in your life? Every theme or trail marker flowing through *Finish Well* is touched by these two words.

## About love

Think about the word "love." Love is multi-faceted like a beautiful gem. Love shows up in patience, kindness, forgiveness, beauty, honesty, joy, trust, peace, hope, intimacy, fun, etc. Picture painted, you understand this. Fear is the other player in the match of life. Fear, too, has many faces. Fear may join with anger, hatred, doubt, selfishness, jealousy, impatience, lying, disconnect, etc. Picture further developed, I trust you see. I ask myself, "How many of love's qualities are in my life or does fear have the better of me?"

These two emotions, actions, and events box with you and me all our days, in the many faces we wear and reflect. Living on love's side is preferable, yes? Is your life flowing from love or fear? Making something immeasurable, measurable, is fun from time to time. We do that all the time, from saying "how" well we enjoyed something (like that was fantastic, instead of good) to "how" awful something was (like saying something was horrible, instead of so-so). Humans are given to calculations, which must be, our rational side being ever present.

In running a good race, you do calculations. It may be fun to do none, and just move along, but you may come to a time in your life when just "floating down the river" and seeing where you go will just not do! Yes, it is a joy to be surprised in life and let things happen, but that is different. That is best done after reason, rationality, and reality have been tapped. Our brains, noted as under used medically, tell me we are made for so much more. I think you want more of what you are made for, too! Living on purpose is what happens to you when you want the facets of love to mark up your frame, and mark up the frame of your life really well.

## About fear

Our world floods our minds with fear. You don't have to look far to be afraid. We worry about our finances, our health, our relationships, and you can fill in the rest of the thought. Fear makes us pay attention, but sometimes it makes us pay too much attention. Fear sells in the marketplace and we buy it. A great fear is fearing that you might fail or fearing that you are inadequate for your dreams. You have already defeated yourself if you find your life here, and it is so far from the truth. Actually, failing is a great gift; you should try it more often. You might even get more out of failing then succeeding. When it comes time for you to succeed, your victories will have been bought from your failures.

I once feared something that has done so much for me — the fear of rejection! I have written for a long time; I have volumes of the printed word in my home. My battle was having the courage to get the work published, but I felt I was not "good enough" and someone could do it better. I also knew writing exposes you to rejection (writing is a naked feeling), which is not something anyone loves. Rejection hurts; you have to have pretty thick skin to face the forms of rejection life tosses at you. What I failed to understand is that when you fear of rejection, it is an invitation to put yourself out to the world. What a change has come from my life when I did that!

Why do we wait so long to do the things we so want to do? Fear of the unknown and untried is one reason. Do we want a life of comfort and ease instead of the reward of work and risk? Few have been made better by ease. Many have been made great by struggle. Someone recently noted to me that laziness and happiness usually do not go together.

When we have lost the ability to respect who and what we are, fear will come to us and tell us we are inadequate. We then have judged ourselves and found ourselves wanting. Respect for your life is critical to respecting anyone else's. I have never met anyone who properly valued their own life treat others poorly. When we have had enough of fear, we can choose to walk with love as our motivator for living. Love, truly is the more excellent way!

How many dreams and attempts were lost to fear before one ever attempted? What if today you had no fears? What would you do differently? This is what your heart asks of you. Will you accept the invitation to press through the obstacles you will face and silence the voice of fear, choosing the portraits of love?

Love, and its effects will be explored in "Love Extravagantly." Fear will be visited again in "Finish Off Fear and Doubt." These two themes run in your race and mine. Only we know how much they have been in the race (maybe someone close to you does, too!). Maybe you have run a race of fear, constantly on guard for the bottom to drop out or never attempting to avoid failure. Maybe you run with love and find a lot of peace on the trail. Now is a great moment, every time, every day, to make more out of what you have and more you can become.

# Chapter Twenty
# The Rhythm of Change and Transition

You can count on some people and things to stay the same, but you can especially count on change and transition. Transition and change are similar, but transition will be known, here, as the process of moving through change. Change is a scary word to many of us. It requires something of us and sometimes we do not wish to obey it. Change is a true constant in our lives. People may fail or succeed in life on how well they flow through change and its transitions.

## Change

So much of what we fear comes from change, from the fear something will change to the fear when change happens. Ironically, much of what creates the joys of life comes from change. Imagine always being thirteen, or forever pregnant, or always living with a broken arm (that would never heal) from an accident? Change makes way for a threshold, passing you to some place, so you can be more and give more.

Change can be, honestly, a very heavy hand. Your kids grow up (can you believe it after all those sleepless nights and mountains of dishes) and leave for college or your spouse dies or you are divorced, and your hope and comfort dies, too. You didn't want it, you didn't plan it, you didn't ask for it — this change — but you got it, and it hurts.

Change may be pushy and force its way upon you, but change always talks to you. One thing it often says is, "Stop and consider for a moment." Change brings you the gift of honest evaluation as it talks. It speaks a little louder, sometimes. Perhaps, you can answer back and say, "I will join you and let you do your work in me." Change can be hated, that is honest, very real, and that is okay.

Wishing things would stay the same is understandable, but keeping life the same is near impossible. Would your child only want to stay an infant, so you could rock them, or would you forever want to be 35 and never see the signs of aging? Could you imagine a world frozen as an infant or at 35? Do you realize how much of life would be missed? How many grandparents could not relive their childhood treats or pass on their wisdom to their grandchildren? Where would wisdom have a place to visit? It is a truth; aging has some benefits that youth does not.

Change can certainly be enjoyed or bring you something you once did not have. A changed flight arrival brought me a hiking buddy and new friend last year. Imagine, one hailstorm in Phoenix, delays our arrival out of Saint Louis, and time brings us together. People and events bring change to our lives, so we might think differently about life, we might do differently, and we might act differently. Who knows the secret mysteries of our lives, we only know that changes and events are no secret.

## *Transition*

Life is walking through many thresholds leading to transition. When the groom does the customary carrying of the bride through the threshold, it symbolizes the passing of one life to another, change and transition. Can you see how this is happening in our own lives? We may not walk through a material threshold but we understand the experience of transition.

Sometimes people give names and stages to transitions, like birth and death. I love the transition symbol of the hyphen in the dates of our lives from birth to death. At a funeral, the speaker mentioned the hyphen was the life lived of the man we were mourning. A hyphen, a life, a threshold, a mark, tells you life has been lived.

Moving through times of transition can be beautiful and hard. They have the opportunity to take us out of comfort zones and into clarity that is beautiful. They bring us out of the common into the unfamiliar. How much of life we would miss if we said, "No, I will pass (trust me, I have wished to pass from time to time or threshold to threshold)?"

When the rhythm and routine, that once brought us security is no longer, transitioning is hard. Children leaving the nest are one transition or putting your son in the hospital for a bone marrow transplant for a month, is another. When you lose someone you love to death, betrayal, change of feelings, or when love isn't enough are difficult transitions. The rhythm of transition feels awful, at times, especially when the outcome is slow or not what we hoped for.

Some transitions are so welcomed. Retirement is, for some. Finally, time to sleep in, or cook, or just do nothing, after years of the every day routine. We have parties for transitions; those we welcome and feel are milestones of living. Where are the parties for the tough transitions? Now one gives a mother who raises children a party when her children leave (or I haven't seen one). How many people throw a "breakup" party when one is transitioning from gain to loss? Having something to symbolize a change or transition is fitting, even in a gesture or symbol.

We transition through many seasons; one of those seasons is aging. We know these seasons come, from the look on our faces, the weight on the scale or the discounts we are available to receive. We smile at some of these times, but these times are transition markers, meaning we are leaving one and nearing another.

We cannot avoid transitions; just as we cannot avoid the change that begins them, they are a part of life. We can recognize they usher in something to bring to our lives and be aware of their benefits. When the kids leave, what will the parents have together? What will they have built over the years? When the job is over, how will the new time be spent? How many of us know people who have finished a significant milestone, and then died. Transitions, tell us something else is coming for another time of growth. That something else comes to us when we open up to it, instead of shut it out.

Don't wish your changes or transitions away. Settle it once and for all; you are where you are to make more of your life, not less. Oh, yes, you can lament them, that is honest. Who would not want some of those moments back? They will always be yours, though. Finding a way to prepare for transitions and change, when you can, and when you can't, will lead you to the finish line, crossing well.

*Finish Well*

# Chapter Twenty-one
# The Opportunity For Men

Men run a different race then women. No kidding, you say. How men view things is usually vastly different than their wife, girlfriend, mother, or daughter. Many of a man's needs are not as different as a woman's, what is different is how those needs are met. An educational course on the differences between men and women could be a relationship saver and way to enjoying a better life. What if a man could get a small view into a woman's world for a minute?

He might find... women love to please on the road of life. In fact, some women will feel this is their greatest purpose in life! Nothing makes them happier than nurturing and sustaining life. A woman will make a choice for others and often not for herself because she is geared to think of others, sometimes over her own needs. She will do this freely, but hope you will do this, as freely and want to find ways to look out for her needs, before she expresses them. When a woman expresses her needs, she wants to be heard, not fixed. A woman can often just talk and be fine with a listening ear.

Sometimes, her pain of not receiving the honor and love she wants will take her to the opposite of what she does naturally. She will find something to fill the pain — food, a relationship, romance novels, and addictions may fill the void. These "fillings" may become substitutes for real pain. Sometimes, they are just coping diversions; sometimes, when honestly looked, at they are not. Life is not that simple, but most every "filling" hides behind some pain.

## Sex begins before the bedroom

Sex starts way before the bedroom with a woman. She bonds with you as you do things for her, play with the children or wash the dishes, and when you let her know she is your number one. She craves intimacy just as much as you; she just develops it in different ways before she shares it with you. A relationship without sexual intimacy is standing on one less table leg. It may stand but it will never stand quite as strong as it could. Getting her to be intimate stems from the differing ways you create it.

You can help her by making sure her needs can be expressed and protected, early on. She might not tell you or say what those needs are, so this is your opportunity to watch for places where she smiles. Then you have a clue to what makes her a woman. In the next chapter we will look at a man's needs, places where a woman can give attention.

## Paying attention before spraying attention

Many women have a hard time drawing boundaries, as to what upsets them and how to express unhappiness in relationships and situations. They may feel it is not lady-like to demand or state needs. When there are problems between you or others, a woman will often let a lot of things go. This is a mistake she thinks she is not making. She may think she is doing the kind thing, but often, the top will pop…later. If a man doesn't pay attention to the smoldering fuse, he will be sorry, and so will she. The periodic bomb goes off and things get said and resolved to some degree. Unfortunately, this cycle will continue if you don't let her feel she has a say in choices and decisions from time to time, and she knows your heart is for her. A heavy hand on a woman based on any system or belief will do both partners very little good.

She is not a mad woman or a crazy one. This is one of the most critically wounding things to say about a woman. She is not crazy because she functions differently than a man. Relationships are so critical to her that most decisions she makes relate to them, for the good of others and the household she nourishes and watches.

## Differing values and design

Men, on the other hand, often make choices for their work or pleasure. This is not bad; it is just a different focus that needs to blend together. Compromise is not merely doing for the other; it is feeling and caring for and about the other. If a man compromises against his will (or a woman for that matter), the solution is no closer to being resolved. Relationships hate fake treaties.

A man on a flight told me his wife helped him secure a great life because he listened to his wife's needs that centered on good relationships and choices for him and the family, even choices he would not have made. He made those choices to trust her because he realized he didn't see things like she did. He felt she was valuable and prized relationships and had more insight into them than he did. He also loved her and valued her heart. He got it and so did the rest of the family, a great family. Women have often been referred to as the cement of relationships. Understanding this will help a man know the need and value of the woman in his life.

It was reported in a seminar I recently went to, it takes a man seven hours to work through difficult and confrontational information presented to him. A woman's brain is much quicker at digesting conflict and applying solutions. She can whip facts and feelings quicker than the sharpest shooter! Your brain, also, is 30% operational at rest, while hers, at rest, is 90% operational! Her mind, in a sense, never stops — making this both an obstacle and opportunity for her gender. I am sure this does not surprise you. She feels deeper and wider, and longer than you. It is easy to see why it often takes some women so much longer to forgive and forget, and recover from heartbreak. It appears to be part of a woman's makeup; she needs to understand her frame and have a man guard her mind from his heart.

Women are verbal creatures and given to believing what you say (at least until they have been betrayed), often because that is how they think and the bonding hormone, oxytocin, moves them along with the desire to connect. I am not saying women don't lie; they can be just as deceitful as anyone, and gender has no prize here. A beautiful thing about women is their desire to give and trust. In fact, a woman friend told me recently, "I lose my happiness if I cannot trust." When a man violates his word to a woman, it is a death to her in a sense. She counted on him and his word. Nobody is perfect, but everybody is best served with honesty and forgiveness.

Lastly, competition fits best at the gym or golf course. Compete only at being the best lover and friend to your wife, girlfriend, and family. If she is a great organizer, praise her, and let her fly. If you cook well, wow, that is awesome; do it gladly. If she keeps the budget better and knows how to keep you out of debt, give her the reins. Complement each other; use your strengths and weaknesses to fill in the gaps, not make gaps. Never crush a woman's dreams or worth through competition or neglect; you will end up paying for it in the long run.

If you desire to finish well, you must pay attention to the racecourse and the racehorse (your lover is more than a horse, but I thought it was a fun compliment). Who you do life with and how you do it will be factors to life's joys. It is nearly impossible to lose a woman by being good to her; you know the flip side, and it is not pretty.

*Finish Well*

# Chapter Twenty-two
# The Opportunity For Women

Women are complex creatures to men. Men are far simpler. Understand this and you have an edge. Each is amazingly (and what a wonder that is) different and the bridge of understanding can seem both narrow and long for both sexes. Woman may vocally ask men to see their side and men may not verbally request the same, but want it all the more. It could happen, if each side realized how different the other's spoken, unspoken, and desired needs are. Negotiating this arena will grow you up, lift you up, or tear you down. Take a look and see if you have been in the school of learning about men.

A man is content to often do almost nothing from time to time, leaving him alone to his happiness and simplicity will make your life easier, and his. Refraining from criticizing him for enjoying this easy delight is another good place to start with him. Pleasure him with this simple understanding, he will love you forever for it. Ask him what pleases him and you will have a good thing going, watch him light up (that is another way to clue in).

A smile and happy heart men find very attractive. The road of life is filled with frowns and sadness. Being real and truly happy, but giving the most of what you have of your life to promoting a peaceful and joyful station in life wherever you are, it will be hard for him to resist. A man can resist a lot of things but a smile and a joyful spirit are easy on his simple mind and matters.

If you are not a happy person naturally, retrain yourself. We all fall on different places on the temperament spectrum and that is the beauty of people. I am a thinker with a more sober and serious look at life, but have a wild pony spirit. I must work more than a happy-go-lucky person to smile and laugh often. Being aware has served me well in most of my relationships. It is not fake; it is making the best of what you are given. People never come in one-size-fits all containers.

## No punishment

Women, don't punish men. This is a dirty little secret. It shows up at a young age. Young men tell me how girls play these little games of "put you in your place" and "punish you" when they did something a girl did not like, even a very minor infraction. This gets you nowhere fast. Since you don't want to go there, right here, becomes an opportunity to be fair and loving more than being right and holding "the grudge." Ouch.

Our minds are more active and it is easier for us to remember our hurts, a recent science article states, but we can choose better by working to be aware of when thinking overwhelms a man and we can't let something go. It will even benefit us, as well. Shutting out a man for his "bad" behavior will shut you out, too. Sorry, it just works that way and no one wins. In fact, most of the time everyone loses.

## More pleasure

Make a man want you. This is not supposed to be a get your guy manual, but removing yourself from him after he has interest, creates an "I want you" that stirs a desire for you. Men can practice this, too. This revolves around creating attraction and desire, the pull and push of wanting and removing. A woman's excessive neediness and too many words will often repeal that which she wants to attract. If she can learn to slow down and enjoy who she is and the place she is in, her relationship can be a place of pleasure rather than so much pain.

A man who loves a woman can learn she is not "bad" for being this way, needy and wordy. This way is part of how her brain is wired and heart is set. A woman thrives on connection. Her way to pleasure is being connected. Some find a man very appealing who plays sports with his children, picks up a dish and takes it to the sink, and is interested in what makes a woman's heart beat. Pretty simple, I would say. It is easier for a man to have his pleasures, often sex, when a woman feels pleasured by these small loving actions. Why, it just works that way. Loving connection is hot.

Expecting so much will lead you to disappointment. Sometimes, no one could hold up to what a woman expects and vice versa with the men. It's no secret that more people are single then married in today's society. Relationships are hard work for most, though some have better chemistry and skills, reducing some of the irritations.

Learn to let some things go (choose wisely), especially irritations that are just that, irritating. Most men will let a problem go, if you don't speak up. It is a burden for them to then have to relive mistakes over and over, when they are slapped in the face with the same issue. This will make a man feel small and wear him down. Men do not do well feeling small. Speak up, at the risk of confrontation, if the issue is worth it, after you have thought about it. You are worth it. He is worth it. Settle it now, and then go on about making a beautiful life.

Here is one of a woman's flaws and grace. Our active brains speak before we think. Woman think and talk, sometimes right off their heads. Women often think a lot as they are made that way. They need those skills to tend to the home and children. Women are often multi-taskers and have focused views on situations. Men would benefit if they got this and patiently dealt with the woman who talks and thinks more than he could ever do in a day. Women need to know their talking and repeating information really gets to them.

Sometimes, it is just because they are busy, but other times their "simple minds" don't like repeated complication. We are far more complicated, but that makes us very interesting. I think this is why men call women crazy — the way women deeply feel, think, and talk. This can be threatening when she only seeks to connect.

We, though, would benefit from speaking and groaning less (did I say that?). The ball is in our court now; disciplining ourselves to exercising a lovely spirit at work or play by speaking up and voting for what you do or do not want in the relationship. It is absolutely okay. I once thought this was not very kind. A man often says what he wants and it is over, communication accomplished. We say what we want and keep saying it, mission just started. Men need a rest from women, not because they do not like them, but because they are not made to communicate like women do.

## *More fun*

Foster a man's passion. If you don't, somebody may. You will tie your heart to a man or child when you learn to love what they love. Enthusiasm for what your spouse, girlfriend, or child loves will pay dividends in the race of life to the finish line. This is a gift that keeps on paying back, even long after your departure from this earth. Loving what someone loves builds a legacy of goodwill and connection. It grows dreams and curbs disappointments.

Take good care of yourself. Nothing new here, but give the best of yourself to this race to the finish. Why go it half-heartedly or sloppily? Yes, you will have times of not being on your best. You may even think, so what? Your man may not think so what, so, love and nurture yourself in how you look and dress. It honestly helps the ride! All relationships have to bend from the ideal. You will hear the burps and snoring, he will get the hair in the shower and shoes and many purses.

*Finish Well*

Life happens; it is not a ride to perfection. I don't want a perfect ride; I want a ride to do the best with imperfect me. This is not selfish; you will make and create happiness for others when you chose to take good care of you. It is the most giving and loving thing you can do. You run the chance of being longer in the race and of doing more good when you care for body, soul, and mind, being more useful to God and others. It just seems selfish and contrary to what we are often taught, but it is the furthest thing from the truth! Read more about this in "Time To Be First."

# TRAIL MARKERS

# Marker 1
# True North, True You

What does being true to you look like? Everyone asked that question, may give a different answer, but one theme would run through the replies — staying the course to who you are and living on purpose the convictions and beliefs you have, without compromising yourself due to someone's influence.

I enjoy beautiful jewelry. I own some, not much, but some. Today we have fakes for almost anything that is beautiful and desirable, very good fakes, might I add. Some of those fakes help us enjoy life, have a little fun, and can be harmless. I enjoy CZs, semi-precious stones, white gold jewelry, and every day steel pieces. It has given me lots of variety to wear and have fun combining and mixing. There is just, still, something beautiful about jewelry that is real, real to the core. Real people are beautiful. Those are the kinds of people that you can't help but love in some fashion or way, even if you may not like them.

The golfer who calls a penalty on himself or the person who admits their error that says, "I want to be true," is very attractive and interesting to me. There is something about the beauty of forgiveness in those people and in other situations where it says, "I take you back and I forgive you." People sometimes are false, because sometimes they cannot be liked any other way, they may not even like who they are. Style instead of substance seems to be their existence, just like some of the materials for fake products today. If they only knew, they are valuable, just like they are.

## Everything is on the line

I see too much of this today, even in close relationships. It breaks my heart that style is practiced without substance, and that is living. It breaks my heart when I am a part of this as well. Finding your true north is a direction to set your compass. It will not be easy. It will take time, a lot of time. It will take tears. It will take love. Love and respect for yourself in spite of everything. Everything you believe, are, love, and hope for, is on the line here. It's not an all or nothing equation, though. No one, absolutely no one, has arrived here, but being true to you is when you have said you want to be on this road and then are attempting every day to walk honestly on it.

Being true to you, it's not being so hard on yourself. It is loving what is unlovable, even if that means you love that part of you or someone else every day. It is finding the good in you and others and celebrating it, not competing against it or criticizing it. Being true is not holding your ground and being stoic, it is laughing. It is working together. It is loving. It is FREEDOM.

True means you don't leave out the obligation of should, but bring in the desire of want to. It means you don't have to, but you will. It means you take you, where you are at, and that person is good enough, no great enough, for the journey, just as they are and will continue to become on the journey. True, signals you are done with the false. Peeling away and putting off are now making time to bring in new clothes. The false may be a good look, just like fake jewelry, but it will never be a satisfying ride. The ride means more than just the appearance to the one who is true.

## Compassion, something priceless to have

Compassion for others is a mark of those who are true to themselves. True people burn very few bridges; they just know they may need to cross them someday. They know telling the truth is only one part of being and living the truth. True, loves the compassion that travels with it, because true knows compassion is what allows a better life for all.

Compassion grows in time, just as a seedling grows into a mighty tree. Expect too much, too fast, you will be looking at little progress and much discouragement. Compassion and the friendship of time have fertilized the heart of those who are true to themselves. Strong and great things grow in time, the beautiful, ever present friendship of time. When being true is more important than appearing true, deep peace takes place inside of you because you finally have nothing to prove to anyone because you proved to yourself who you really are.

*"Above all be true to yourself; if you can't put your heart in it, take yourself out of it."*

# Marker 2
# Love Extravagantly

You read that right. Whatever it costs you, love. Love is the risk of everything that is precious to you. Your hope and dreams are wrapped softly in love. You can be safe and stay arms length with love, but then that kind of safety is very risky. I've been hurt. You've been hurt, too, or you haven't loved. Loving extravagantly is the most reasonable way to live because it makes life worth being here!

Never be cynical about love. Yes, it can wound you, elude you, and pain you, but it is worth all roads to travel, all bridges to cross, all mountains to scale and all reasons to find. Love is the word and it is a BIG word. Oceans could not fill the desires, needs, and thoughts found in love. Writers and lovers have long sought to capture it, but love is greater than the ability to harness it. Love is just that great and experiencing love is even greater.

Closing yourself from love, because of the possibility of hurt, would close you to the possibility of love's pleasure. You may be safe, but you will more than likely be alone and lonely. One of the ways to find safety in love is to love and value who you are first, knowing how you tick and respond in life. So much of our insecurities are exposed in loving, it is good to be progressing and arriving at the place of self-respect and self-love early and always in life.

## Love is one amazing and worthwhile ride

Love is found in many places, people, and ways across the spectrum of life. You can love a family member, a friend, a place or a favorite item. You can love more than one person, at the same time, though you may love them differently. Your heart may try to quantify love, but the quality of it cannot be quantified, except by continual expression.

Love is fathomless, yet, it is written about to attempt to explain and hold it. There is no driving force like love. It keeps people questing to secure it or wanting to die, when it is absent. Who can forget Daniel Day Lewis, as Hawkeye, in *The Last of the Mohicans*, as he spoke this stirring and passionate message to Cora when they had to part, "You stay alive, no matter what occurs! I will find you. No matter how long it takes, no matter how far, I will find you."

I have learned a great secret in life (please pass it around). Those you love become beautiful. There are no unattractive people who and when you love. When you tie your heart with someone, something magical happens… you get new vision. You no longer see with natural vision, you see deep and farther than possible to behold. Love is when two are just better together than they would ever be separately.

Love is all it is cracked up to be. It is so worth it, though you may experience great pains to secure it. You may be poor, but you will never ultimately be poor if you loved or are loved. The richness of love adds a value to living that no money could ever secure. This is why love is an unquenchable quest to find what is worth spending all your days for. We are all flawed, but oh, the joy to sparkle in someone's eyes.

People are pleased to be remembered we love them, and happy when we show them. Life will never run out of opportunities to do this for the beloved. There will never be enough lifetimes when you love because love's desires and expressions fill more than a lifetime. We can enjoy this journey, of loving, through all the woes and storms that land on our quest.

## Don't dismiss your feelings

Love makes you feel, but it is far more than a feeling. Being so done with books that express love as an act, without regard to how you feel has tired me. (I do believe in this part of love absolutely, but it is only one part of love.) There is a book someone gave me at a very low time, called, Feel. It was not the status quo book on life, and I appreciated its fresh honesty. Too much of modern society has gotten into our souls, teaching us to dismiss how we feel. You and I feel and feelings will always accompany us on life.

Don't dismiss how you feel, ever. If you can learn to appreciate and discern how and what you feel, you will finish well. If you take your heart with you in life's places (not merely your head), you will never be betrayed by yourself. You feel because, you think. If you want to feel differently, you need to think differently. Do not ask yourself to feel what you do not believe.

Love is the greatest motivator in the world. Want to make someone motivated for the right reasons? Love them. Show them love, by what you say, ask, and do. Study what makes them smile and find ways to create more smiles. A good craftsman never fails to learn more about his trade and product, so he can make a finer product. Love is like this; it can be beautifully crafted and shaped in your hands and heart.

When you know you are loved, there is a security net that allows you to leap into life. You know you always have a safe place to fall, when you are loved. Many of the world's ills could be solved, if love was the ointment to the wounds. When we do not love, the world starves a little.

## Risk everything for love

Risk everything for love, though it may be costly. Even life with love will have some thorns, as a quote I once read. Throw away the talk that love does not bring pain or hurt. Too many articles I read say this. True, in love's perfect form, but send me over someone who has ever loved like that. Loving involves the opportunity for pain and being inconvenienced. Someone once told me, "Love is the willingness to be inconvenienced for somebody." Though we wish for this perfect love, if we are willing to learn from love, we will be "perfected" in it through all the turns and twists of pursuing it. As the quote follows, "A life empty of love will have no roses."

Love means never having to say you are sorry, but ALWAYS being willing to. In the humanness of our souls we truly fail to love, in the deepest sense of the word. We know that, without anyone telling us. Since we know that, we will understand the need to repair what has been lost in our relationships. We will secure love's vigor, trust, and honor to those we most care about, when we can open our mouths and hearts to find the words, "I have wronged you, I am truly sorry." Only the ones you love and the ones you want to love you can hurt you. All the others only cause you irritation.

Love's offer is in the extravagant living of it. You cannot enjoy love cautiously. Love cannot be thwarted, in the sense that you can love in spite of everything, if you choose. Difficult yes, but love always brings the possible. Love does not know it cannot win. Don't be cynical or long discouraged, love is worth everything it is thought to be… and then some.

*"Love is not blind—it sees more, not less. But because it sees more, it is willing to see less."*

*Finish Well*

# Marker 3
# Finish Off Fear and Doubt

Has fear ever made you make a decision? You are probably laughing and thinking, well, of course I have. Do you realize how many dreams and hopes have been lost because of fear? I know of a child who was aborted because of fear, though nothing was ever found to be wrong with the child.

I know of men who competed in a sport and just couldn't finish what they started because of fear. I have heard of people who lost their lives because of fear. Fear is powerful stuff that can destroy everything your life is built upon. Some of us are one step away from a disaster, and we know it. We know we don't have the resolve to take one more blow or one more bad report. Fear of what could be, ruins the possibility of what might be.

I have been a near expert on this, in the past. Oh, not all the time and in all things, but fear (from what I read, was told, etc.) got the best of me so I could give the worst of me. That is what fear does. Nothing good, absolutely nothing good comes from fear, unless you decide it can't have you anymore. Fear is a thief; come to rob you again and again. I have never found one benefit of fear, except it shows you that you must change the way you think (unless it is fear of something that can harm you, like fire).

How many dreams were lost to fear? How many ideas or new products were never developed or seen to completion because of fear? How many lives perished and how many people cried for relief of fear's wake? We will never live a life without fear, but we can always live a life with less fear. There are oodles of tips and stories about conquering fear, but the best one I have found is to think of what you love to do and be found doing it!

Not madness and endless motion, but purposeful joy runs with you when you love the station you are in or want to be in (or you are working to be in). Fear is usually greatly exaggerated in the mind, where you and the media create a life out of it. Finish it once and for all, and then, daily; make steps to run without fear. Run the race with the purpose and passion you feel designed for. Taking the time to find out what makes you thrive is worth everything. It is not easy (there are a lot of things to fear) but fearing fear is the worst fear. As my co-worker shared with me, "The greatest fear is to fear you are incapable of reaching your dreams."

## Put down doubt

Finish off doubt, just like someone would do in a sporting match, when they finish an opponent (as in match play in golf). Get doubt down and then get it out! Doubt breeds when you do nothing. One way to succeed is to

## Finish Off Fear and Doubt

accept that some doubt is woven in the fabric of life; there are no answers to some of our questions, hard as we try or agonize.

Finish off doubting yourself. When we are young, we may be fearless, but we can doubt our abilities. We need patience to realize we are in the school of learning and we will be for a long, long time. We also doubt our looks (girls especially do this, though not foreign to boys) and critic others and ourselves unmercifully. Stop it now or wherever... at 30, 40, or 50. You have what you need; you have what is good for your life. You are more than adequate than you can imagine. You bring something no one else brings to life. Embrace it and develop who you are. I know this more than ever at the second half of my life. I love the weathered and the worn me. I am seeing more things I am than I am not, and there is something nice about that in life.

Stop doubting what you know. If you are not sure about something, find knowledge and do something with it! Talk to others. Go to school, learn, develop. Information can be skewed, but be a searcher. We will never know the best car, the best doctor, the best church, the best man, etc. Those things can be subject to opinion. Think more on what is "wonderfully" adequate or excellent instead of always looking for the "most" of everything. It doesn't exist, at least not all the time and in all things. Yes, some information, products, and ideas are better than others, but even "the lesser" ones may accomplish your aims, instead of the quest to be ideal in acquiring both information and items.

Operate under the best information you can at the time you decide or use the information and let that be enough for the journey.

Finish off doubt at what you do not know. I do not know the day I will die. I think about it from time to time, but I cannot enjoy life if I am thinking too much on it. I do not know every thought that God has about every subject and situation. I will not understand why life is easier or more difficult for some than others. It just is; you don't have to understand it all to do well.

In my youth someone said once, "Be afraid of nothing but sin." I have to say that is a pretty good thought. That is easy, on one hand, and since we are all human, not so easy on the other. We know we don't get all of life right. We only know today is an opportunity to get some of it right with the way we think and the choices we make. This is your opportunity to finish well and finish off fear and doubt.

*"Only when we are no longer afraid do we begin to live."*

# Marker 4
# Say It, Do It

This is one of my favorite things...a challenge with action. This is a way you may use obligation to work for you instead of guilt you. Say you are going to do something and do it — follow through. You have told people and they are on notice and so are you! This is a great motivator to get something done.

Only two words of caution come through. Did I guilt you? It was not spoken to make you feel bad. It was to encourage you, what you say has power. Be as good as your word and be even better. Don't let me leave you with the impression perfection is the only way to your word and seeing it through is the only way to finish. It is not; we must quest to do our best. If we are honest, we haven't from time to time, but we can find a way to begin anew.

When you tell someone you are going to do something, plant that little seed in your mind and see it through. It will be something to strive toward and something to see accomplished. I love the Michael Jordan quote, "You have to expect things of yourself before you can do them."

Thinking of what you should or could do before you do something will help you do it. Meaning, be there, before you are. Oh, and yes, be there, before you are and you have a great opportunity to, BE there.

## Follow through

You will never get away from taking care of business, cleaning, and upkeep. Never. These are givens. We are caretakers in many domains. We can't do everything, but we can do something. When you tell someone you are going to call them or return that email, find a way to get back to them in a timely manner. Even if that timely manner has passed, get back to them. It is good for you and for them to make the circle of completion. People like resolution and taking care of things is a way help you get things accomplished; now enjoy the follow through.

There are endless ways to follow through in life. I have started many projects I have never finished. It is embarrassing to say that, but very honest. You might even find yourself here at one time. People admire those who are good for their word. We know we will not get this finally and totally right in our lives, but saying what you want to do, can be that push to make you do something. Then you get the pleasure of seeing something done. Completion is part of the celebration and beauty of life, even as a setting sun completes the day.

You can ask someone to hold you accountable and wow, will that be fun! When I mentioned I was doing something that had a deadline, people would come up to me and ask, "How is that project you said you were doing coming along?" It was good for me to find checkpoints to where I was or what I was doing. It was also great, as an evaluation, to see if I was serious about what I said and meant.

You get to see what is important to you when you use your words. Speaking them and then doing are ways to put your dreams and desires in place. Now, they are out there and you get to answer back. When you want to finish well, say it and do it.

*"The biggest problem in the world could have been solved when it was smaller."*

*Finish Well*

# Marker 5
# Caution Ahead

The big three — and we are not talking about auto companies! If ever I have tumbled, here is a place where I keep watch and am more aware of my failings. One thing I have sadly learned is that WE can and do MISUNDERSTAND those we care for and love, we can even be judges to them. It is just the very imperfect lives we give to each other. Many friendships have been damaged and marriages broken by assumptions, judgments, and expectations.

There is a time to "mind your own business." When is the difficult time I recently read something by Byron Kate that stated there are three kinds of business: yours, God's, and mine. Refreshing knowing, what is your business, will be a guide for what you do with the big three. It is not so easy because our lives cross, intersect, and brush each other's.

When we are involved in some else's business, it is much easier to assume, judge, and expect. You will find as you experience life that each of us bring different perspectives and histories to the gathering table of life. Trying to be compassionate (and walking in their moccasins), both to others and yourself, will serve as another guide to getting this right.

## Guarding what is good

These three move subtly in our lives and we sometimes don't even consciously realize we have formed opinions in their processing and nailed others without a fair trial. Sometimes an assumption or judgment becomes a truth to us, even if it is or was a lie. Guarding against these three, as you would guard your life, will save you so much relational distress and hard thinking of others. More trouble is born out of these deadly three than any other threes I can think of. Life is truly not fair, and sometimes we are the ones who are not fair. Being AWARE and honest about right perceptions is so important It can save you years of heartbreak.

If you love someone in great measure, you must especially guard against assuming. Assuming is on the prowl to think the worst or fear the worst. Sometimes a conflict is not as bad as you can make it be! Judgment is a verdict rendered without all the facts and with consequences. When our hearts are hardest or less vigilant, our judgment is most skewed. A softer heart filters mercy into matters. I love the quote, "Judge the size of a man's shoe, not the size of his heart." How much pain has entered our lives and the lives of others when we have chosen the path of judgment without right information? If we are honest, we might find we are the ones who could do better, before we would point the finger at someone else.

Expectations are future hatreds. Everyone has them, expectations, that is. We expect life to go a certain way. In fact, we do things so life will go a certain way, the way we expect it, and it does not. We cannot secure our lives even with right behavior and then expect them to turn out the way we wish, but right behavior may save us from other difficulties. How many times have you been mad when you expected something of someone? Were you ever surprised in a good way, when you expected something bad of someone and they did something better than you expected?

Expectations are unpredictable and they set you up for pain, much pain. Finding ways to have reasonable expectations, and ones that will not break you, when those expectations are not happening, lets you relax along the way and enjoy the good stuff!

These three in life trip us all up on the race to finish well. Being aware of the obstacles in your race will let you keep watch more diligently. Watching is a position of strength and we all need more of that on the way to the finish line.

*"Good judgment comes from experience, and experience—well, comes from poor judgment."*

*Finish Well*

# Marker 6
# That's the Way It Is — or Is It?

When two things are opposite, how can you believe them both to be true? We say, "That's the way it is." Well, maybe it could have been different. Life often has two sides that can be true, but at different times. Look ahead, but there is a time to look back; it is just a matter of when and why, is one of them. Love may mean stand up, there is a time to say I won't do that, which is just as loving and kind when the time calls for it.

Life brings us perspectives from several sides and people often find themselves on one side or the other. It may be easy to take the fatalistic or destiny view in life and say, if it is meant to be, it will be. I had once heavily placed my life on this side, but not in the same way in recent years. I cannot know providence's favor and guide, but I have the steering wheel for some things in life. Maybe, it is like my husband would say when I use to get nervous on a flight. (Let me bring you your steering wheel!) I think I am controlling something, though I am really not.

We do not know what we control, but we do have some control. Where control ends or begins, I cannot name, but I am participating in life rather than letting life happen. Everyone will have a different look at this, all are found at different places on how life is lived.

## Cash in on life

Just for a minute, imagine someone gave you a million dollar check. You take it and put it in your wallet, but you never cash it. You don't trust the person who gave you the check; you didn't think it was real or enough, so you never cash it. What will the check do for you? Probably nothing, but occupy space in your wallet and maybe conversation, when you show it to someone. You were given "life" in a sense and you told the bearer the terms of it. How much difference might your action have made in the cashing or depositing of the check? Plenty, plenty of life could be lived with the cashing of it, and the cashing in of your life.

Fear plays its game with us, the fear of not being enough. Instead of taking what you have and doing something with it, you do nothing to better your station. That is so far from the truth; you are more than enough. Sure you could be better, smarter, prettier, etc., but you cannot be more ready than today to want to be all you can become! Today is that first movement, that first changed thought, that first dance, that first step, toward succeeding

So you want to meet that cute girl or guy, but you wait till she notices you or gives you the signal. You want that job, but you pass on getting more knowledge or listening for your weaknesses and addressing them, so you can be more marketable and seasoned. In the years of my life, I have seen more people hope, and less people do.

I have been there. Hope is great, but doing is where the action and life is. Life seems to fall in the laps of those who want it and work for it. It just seems to look like luck or providence, but hard work and success has often followed the break and opportunity it created. Yes, I see magic and unexplained things happen, people getting found or their budding abilities taken and worked with, but most of the time, you need to show up and sail through.

As you are on your way, interesting things happen. I don't know how, and I don't care how. It just does and it is so fun to dance with it. Did I make my life or did life make me? I can't say, but I do know, when I got in the dance, suddenly the songs I wanted to dance to came on!

Don't wish, wait, and do nothing, hoping for a rescue from somewhere. Act, improve yourself, have confidence, and yes, hope in God. But when your ship comes in, get on it, and be the best sailor you can be. Only then will you find out where it could take you!

*"Experience is the hardest kind of teacher. It gives you the test first and the lesson afterward.*

*Finish Well*

# Marker 7
# Confidence Grows Here

Confidence is just one of many trail markers of good finishers. It is one so vital and interwoven in all the other good marks of finishing well. Without it, we stand on shaky ground. With it, buildings are made, pitches turn into home runs, books get written, and ventures get taken. All the places confidence can take you, you want to be there.

One magazine recently quoted a celebrity saying, "Confidence makes you more desirable." That may be an understatement. Confidence is not easily secured by most of us. Confidence usually comes from failing, as much as it can come from succeeding. It is just what heart you have inside you that determines the difference. I have seen very attractive people feel unconfident and those not as attractive, be very confident. So what is the magic of confidence?

Confidence is playing to your strengths while you recognize your weaknesses or limitations, while you enjoy life! It is making much of what you have and being thankful for it. It is working diligently with the portion you were given and creating a masterpiece with it! That girl may have a winning smile and joyful laugh, and she learns how to use it with people to create love and friendship. The short man may even laugh about his stature, but when it comes time to lead a company or see a project through, he has the "it" factor in confidence!

## Confidence calls

Through the growing years of life and the way we see ourselves in the world, confidence either ebbs or flows based on our perceptions and experience. Confidence can be a vicious cycle; sometimes you need it, to get it. Sometimes to get it, you need it! I have watched merciless collapses in golf tournaments. Those I don't soon forget. A large lead evaporates, an unusual happening, and suddenly a good walk is spoiled.

Why does someone so capable fall apart? Many times it is confidence, the feeling of being settled is not working within you. You often will believe, you belong, where you belong. Today, you felt like you didn't belong in the winner's circle or couldn't shoot that low score, so you don't. We so often rise to where we think we can, and land where we think we should be.

Rejection can actually be an aid for confidence. It grows something inside of you, by trying again, by mastering something, as long as you do not get too discouraged. When you learn to master more of what is in you, you will gain confidence. As you keep desire alive and use your skills, time will add confidence in your work and world.

Relational success thrives with confidence. Insecurity and jealousy chip away at confidence, both for you and others When you can be comfortable in your own skin, you have the best opportunity to be humble, yet, be confident. Wanting something too much can put the pressure on your confidence, unless you are convinced in your mind, you should be there. I see this all the times in sports, and in a winner — they believe they belong — and they perform accordingly.

*"Low self-esteem is like driving through life with your hand brake on."*

*Finish Well*

# Marker 8
# Find Creativity and Contentment

Just look around you and you will see the product and fruit of creativity. I marvel everyday with the amazing things I see and use. Even this computer that prints this type amazes me. Wow, have we seen some creative products and things in our lifetime. Creativity opens the soul. We are so, so we create. I think this is how we boldly proclaim we are made in the image of God — the desire and joy of creating.

Doing what you love and keep doing it speaks creativity's message. As a dear friend once told me, "Love God and do whatever you like." I like that! How sad to work at a job for money and benefits alone. I admit life is not perfect, but to live a whole life like this is, well, sad. Being brave and "changing horses," when this looks like your legacy offers a way to make room for your creative expression. Learning how you can find something you love to do, make a living at it or learn to ride real close to what brings you pleasure and uses your gifts, spells, joy and success for most of us.

Everyone is creative, only it is expressed differently. I see and work with creative people every day. I see it in teamwork. I see it in respect. I see it in the appreciation of our differences, not merely similarities. Those who are different are teachers to those willing to listen, echoing the sentiment, "If two people are both alike, then one of them is unnecessary." A creative spirit is enhanced by what is different and unfamiliar. All the forces that move us along life's corridor do so from being near people and things unlike us. We will never be who we are without differences. Look at how different the same sunset can be painted!

The old adage, form follows function, speaks well for creativity. The need for products that serve cause minds to create them. Buildings in their many shapes and patterns go up with the architect's creative imagination. Yearbooks walk students out of school with images and views from creative minds and methods. The world is birthed in creation every day from the minds, hearts, and hands of creation.

While you are creating, create a well of good friendships and good will to those around you. A person who finishes well will do well with friends, good friends and even just nice acquaintances. Quality is better than quantity, but have both if you can. Be good to those who mean the most to you (not implying be less to others), don't take their presence for granted and the things they do for you. Human tendency seems to find this road of "taking for granted" too easily.

## Contentment calls

One of my favorite books on contentment, written over 350 years ago, is by a man named Jeremiah Burroughs. His simple book, *The Rare Jewel of Christian Contentment* has left me spellbound over the ages. It is simple, honest, understandable, yet challenging. He notes that contentment is a sweet, inward disposition of the heart and how precious this "jewel" is, but not always easily secured.

We will probably never, at the same time, have all we wished for in life. We may never have what we so long to have, but the act of finding contentment, seasons well on the way to finish well. Difficult, sometimes, maybe it seems even impossible at times. I enjoy watching animals rest; they are usually very contented. This picture of them is comforting. We are so much better when we are contented and creativity best comes forth. Contented, yet striving, but not satisfied to stop excelling. There is a fine line between the two, but you can have lack, yet strive and still be content.

Contentment makes the sunset sweeter, the sitting on the porch more memorable, and the marriage more agreeable. Contentment is taking your problems, wanting them (in the sense you keep yours and I keep mine) and working with them, as someone once tried to explain to me. It's not that things were the way you liked them, it is just they were what you had, and finding a way to take what was good, is possible while you have them.

Creativity's expression flows out of loving what you do and letting it do its work. When you enjoy what you do, you bring the possibility of contentment that closer to grasp.

*Finish Well*

Satisfying and pleased are words that mirror contentment. Creating a life begins with respect of who you are with the mission you are assigned. Writing, life all over where you go, is one of life's creative and uncomplicated pleasures on the way to finishing well.

*"Most people are content with old problems, rather than new solutions."*

# Marker 9
# Affectionately Yours

Signing a letter with a loving closing is a fitting way to end one. Affection is an essential way to travel. You can store up affection from receiving it, you can give it, you can enjoy it, and you can fight for it!

It comes to you and me in many ways. A card, a word or words, an action or a gesture or even in ways you may never know (I so enjoy when someone, even after a great amount of time has gone by, tells me they have thought of me or loved me while we were apart). Affection creates connection and bonds you to another

There is no debate—affection is good for you. Research shows that the endorphin release from a 20-second hug can produce wellbeing, and it is no secret that good sex can prolong your life! That is courtesy of God; He made it that way! Those health studies show deep interpersonal relationships guard your health, just as much, if not more than foods. This is no secret; every heart gets this and who wouldn't want this?

The simple pleasures shared, like a kiss, a hug, or intimate touch and connection, brings the best of life to you. Be extravagant in affection on this one, give and share yourself with those who matter to you. Being the first in this department is a bonus for you (see the others in Be First). I don't have to see your affection as public display, but tender public affection has never tired me and has often encouraged me to be more affectionate.

## You should be kissed often

I never lose interest in seeing someone hugging at the airport or kissing upon arrival, even goodbyes have loving gestures. I do this all the time and I am so glad I am getting better at it! On many of my runs or walks I find people kissing at the park. I don't find this offensive; I find it living passionately As Rhett Butler said to Scarlett in *Gone With The Wind*, "Your problem is you should be kissed, and you should be kissed more often." I agree. Kissing is such a pleasurable event. Those are some of the "best in life" free gifts.

One of my favorite places for affection is at bedtime (made you wonder). I have long enjoyed sitting next to my son and rubbing his back and head as we talk, and he falls asleep. I have done this since he was born and, as long as I have life and he asks for it, I will be there. Have you ever had the privilege of someone falling asleep from your comfort? It is bliss. We will never know how much our hearts are tied when we do this.

Watching attraction and romance is fun; being involved in it is ecstasy. Stories like *Romeo and Juliet* and

*The Last of the Mohicans* remind me of affection, passion, and deep loving, making affection worth "fighting" for. Who doesn't want to be that girl who gets the "fighting affection" especially when she wants it? Affection can play into rejection when it is not reciprocated. That is painful and most of us have had some lessons on that kind of pain. It will never stop me, though, because affection is a way of living, not just what you do!

Taking care of someone who is ill offers amazing moments of affection, even in trying times. Watching my mother love my father in his closing days was a beautiful thought and sight I will never forget. It tied the whole family together. My husband's watch at his mother's bedside will forever be engraved in my mind. I saw something of him; I loved seeing in the measure he offered. Affection with those you live and breathe life with will create a sweet legacy long after you or they are gone.

Have I made you want to hug or kiss someone? Very good, that is the writer's joy, moving you to ponder and action. Those who finish well make a whole lot of room for affection on the journey and they get the pleasure, as well as those pleasured.

*"Love is the life of the heart."*

*Finish Well*

# Marker 10
# Live Your Own Life

It is so tempting to want to control an outcome, even the outcome of another's life. Parents do this all the time by living on edge of "what might happen" to their child. So they "manage" outcomes. There can be a fine line between guidance and control. We can want "the best" but we do not always know how that will come about. Surely some of life's lessons are painful and learned no other way than through pain. Is saving someone from the choices they make in their life the answer?

When we stop manipulating others, we can do what we need to do and they can do what they must. A sail never controls the sea; it only lends itself to operate within the waters. We can set the sails on our ships, yet, still never have full control of the waters. You may think you are helping someone get somewhere when you set his or her sails, but you are creating directional confusion.

Children leaving the home are one of life's most painful transitions. The common and every day routines are forever changed when college appears. Everything is different, from the missing place setting, to the amount of wash in the basket. Lost is a new word for mothers who have not prepared for this journey they now find themselves on. Even those who thought they were prepared, this place on the journey takes them to places they have never known. The desire to fix and influence disrupts the departure of the birds that must fly.

## No fixing and rescue, please

We try to rescue instead of support, cage instead of fly. I don't doubt that saving someone from their choices may make your life easier, but the pitfalls of growth for both people are enormous. The need to fix and rescue has slowed the train down and dropped people at foreign destinations. You may think you are getting somewhere quicker and with less woe, but there are prices to pay, if not now, later.

A young man's father once told me his son reached a crisis. He had bailed out his son so many times and then came the time he could not bail him out. The father realized he never let his child live his life and figure out some of his challenges on his own. He didn't want his son to struggle, so he came to his aid, but things caught up with everyone.

Dreams die slow deaths when we don't allow others to live their own lives and you, yours. We only have so much energy to give in this life, and knowing what is your responsibility and what is not is a great help in finishing well. When you have adopted a responsibility that is not yours, you have diverted energy from your purpose.

Consequently, the other person who has not lived his life has missed out on where they are and what they need to do.

Sharing and caring about other people's lives is life at its best, but invading ground that is theirs to till makes for a disorganized garden that was meant to flower and array in its own season of life. Living your own life is far more manageable and will allow you to give attention to what needs attention. You might even be surprised what you will accomplish and the satisfaction you will experience when you live your own life.

*"Life is often like a sprint—long stretches of hard work punctuated by brief moments in which we are given the opportunity to perform at our best."*

*Finish Well*

# Marker 11
# Express Gratitude for Wounds

That's right, you read it correctly. Can we say thank you to who or what has wounded us? This is a hard one, I understand the why, it is just the how that is so difficult. Being thankful for the pain received shows where you are on the road. As you work through the hurt, you get so much from the lesson and will keep getting out of the lesson. This place is empowering as you "get it." I vacillate back and forth between acceptance and anger, but those two steps back seem to be leading many steps forward. Slowly, but slow is progress and hope in the race of life.

I love to hike. It is here where I think, cry, pray, and sing. You can find me in one of these positions at some place on my hikes. Recently I hiked with a friend who told me something her preacher father told her, "That which you can be thankful for, no longer has the power to wound you." The thought hit me. One reason I was not thankful is because I could not accept the pain. As I have learned to be thankful for the pain and realize it was in my life to do me good, I can at least swallow the idea of that thought! It never negates that I hurt, it only asks me to consider that the work of pain has more purpose than I can imagine. A great challenge has been set for me!

People can be irritating; some can exasperate you. Here in the school of life, you get lots of opportunities to find irritation or gratitude. Irritating people actually provide indicators, showing us where we need some fixing ourselves. That traffic jam, that makes you want to explode or the nasty tape register change, when you are most in a hurry, all get to season you for living more gratefully. We think we have reached our limits with that child or spouse, when one day we look back and realize we (and they) have grown through what irritated us. Progress!

## Expressing gratitude for wounds can make you better

I know a man who said someone mercilessly picked at him on his job. He vowed to use the time to make his life better and to be a better man. Wow! I don't know if that would have been my motivation, but I sure like it. It challenges me. Too many things once easily irritated me, but I have moved ahead, learning some of these great lessons.

So much is written about the attitude of gratitude these days. It is difficult to feel gratitude every day and in every situation. We should honestly give room to others and ourselves when we are below the standard we hope to be.

*Express Gratitude for Wounds*

Feeling guilty for not being thankful is nonproductive and probably won't get you to gratitude sooner. Behind it all, being thankful for good and beauty has no down sides and we all have so much of it in our lives, even in our struggles. Besides, gratitude is part of the transforming work done in our souls, sometimes in ways we do not realize as we go through the process of pain.

It is pretty safe to say you will be happier, healthier, and more hopeful when gratitude visits your heart and face. It is far easier to embrace and love someone who is grateful. Gratitude makes us more fun to be around.

Watching those who have found this "secret" work in operation is fascinating. I mentioned Mattie before. His smile, his love, and his GRATITUDE were so amazing for someone wheelchair bound and life infirmed, proving again that gratitude has power to change, not only the person grateful, but also the person on whom it falls! A good finisher knows grateful is not just a destination; it is a way to travel.

*"Life may not be the party we hoped for, but while we're here we should dance."*

*Finish Well*

# Marker 12
# Find Your Voice

What is your voice? We all have one, even those who cannot speak. Your voice is the part of you that is who you really are and who you present to the world. Seems fairly simple, doesn't it? It is not.

Your voice is sometimes the last thing heard when you speak or communicate. Finding your voice does not come easy to some. When you are growing up, you are always being taught how to use your voice by the way you behave and think. Too much correction and "guilting" can make one want to hide their voice for fear of disapproval. Sometimes we even hide from what we believe about God. We sense that our voice must be expressed a certain way, even if we feel vastly different or ambiguous about that voice.

A woman shared that when she was in a group setting, it was hard for her to listen to her voice when she was speaking. Speaking up was scary to her. People who find their voices, without trampling over other's voices, are good finishers in life. They often lead, know what they want, and can get what they want because they do not fear the sound of their voice, the expression of who they are. It is more than confidence; it is value. Valuing the pulse of your heart and the expressions it brings lends to your voice.

Bringing the best of you comes with showing up with your voice. How can you communicate what you want unless you know your voice? How can you know what you want unless you find your voice? The exercise of this takes time, sometimes years. It is the quiet confidence that you are all right with yourself and your beliefs.

## My, what a voice can say

When you find your voice, it will be difficult for those who have not found theirs. You might be considered bossy, disagreeable, or inflexible. Don't believe this, if you can present your voice with kindness and grace. When you find your voice, you no longer will be afraid if someone disagrees with you. It will not make you change who you are and what you want. You will not sense the need to challenge them because you know what is good and right, rather than what is confrontational and dictatorial. You will desire peace instead of war when your voice is from the correct place.

Women may take years to find their voice because their nature is to please and follow. This is a beautiful place for a loved woman, but even more beautiful when others love her with her voice and let her freely offer it. Children will find no downside in a mother with a voice, even when she uses it to instruct, inspire, and stand up for what is good and better. Her voice will help her children be examples in society of decisiveness and courage.

Men are supposed to have a voice (culturally we still find patterns that do not always do us good because truth applies to all sexes, not one or the other), so this is often already expected of them. They can suffer silently when they do not feel the power of their voice. Growing and finding courage to face old patterns and truths will help bring out the voice within, as surely as loving, respect and acceptance. A man who is secure is strong, but a man who knows his voice will never abuse his strength. His voice will only enhance his strength.

A proper voice is respectful to all men and women, but it does not waiver when it is not welcomed. Finding your voice is like finding true north; you will always have a point of origin. That voice knows, by standing, everyone is made better and accountable, even the person who knows his voice.

*"I must do something" will always solve more problems than "something must be done."*

*Finish Well*

# Marker 13
# Remember and Reminisce

How precious to us is memory; without it, hearts are lost or broken. The recent attention to Alzheimer's and dementia brings memory into the foreground. You cannot escape the pain that a lost memory brings, both to the person with it and to those who love them. Memory is also a sweet salve when the present is difficult, as it can be at any time.

When my father was ill and suffering from an illness that also affected his mind, it was heart breaking to watch. My smart, capable engineering father could not read instructions on a toy information sheet on Christmas. I was stunned the first time I witnessed this. Then came more times to break my heart. I remember once when he was looking at photos in the hallway of the three of us girls and he exclaimed to my mother, "Those are pretty girls; are they yours?" They were his, very much his, but he had lost the ability to know that. Little did I realize, how much comfort is lost when you have lost the ability to remember.

Reminisce is the word; remembering is the means. We do it all the time. We are looking forward to a reunion or a gathering, so we can reminisce. We join to remind ourselves what we shared with them at a past time and place. We then get to make new memories all over again, so we can reminisce another time! A reunion is fun to have others jog your memory from time past and, in a sense, fill in the gaps with you of things you forgot, that you love hearing again.

## Reminisce...taking pictures

Taking pictures is a lasting way to remember and reminisce. Today, there is absolutely no excuse for not taking pictures. You can get a picture from just about anywhere — a cell phone, a pocket camera, or a full size camera. Wow, if a picture paints a thousand words, today's products can do ten thousand! If you own a computer, picture keeping has never been easier and more enjoyable. The world of photography has always been exciting, but never more than today. At your fingertips are ways to keep your memories alive.

I have heard it said, "I have the picture in my mind." That is wonderful and a mind is a great place for a picture. A photograph, though, will sharpen the details the mind has faded. Just tonight, I saw pictures on a long ago trip to London. I remember the hotel well, but until I saw the pictures, I realized I didn't remember it quite as well as I thought. Creating a photo book has been a new delight. Priceless memories, right on the coffee table, on demand, is the place you can find the people and places you have seen and walked through life alongside.

## Reminisce...not easy at times

Remembering can be very painful, like the loss of a child or a terrible accident. I just travelled with someone who lost her father to fire. She was still sorting through the pain of his death, but remembering the love and deep joy she will always have for him in her life. "Sometimes the sweetest and most enduring memories we have are of those who are no longer a part of our lives," writes Kathy Crawly.

The past has stored up for you treasures to take out and look at again. There are even things about the past that are painful that can be worth another look. You can look at the past differently and be thankful for what it taught you. One of the great gifts of the past is savoring some of the sweetness, even in the bitterness of it. The past is not only meant to hurt you, but to heal you.

No one forgets the past unless you have memory problems. The past serves up something to us and for us. What exactly, we do not fully know, but in time some things get explained, and sometimes we just get more peace and resolve. Travelling well on the road of life pays attention to the present place you are on with a reach to the future, but it welcomes you to a glance back to check on a fellow runner or position you find yourself on the road. One of the ways to run well is to run with the pleasure of the joys you have, had, or learned. That is found in the place of reminiscing. Don't leave the past behind; everything it has brought you is for you, not against you.

*"Remember me and smile."*

*Finish Well*

# Marker 14
# Remember To Be Kind

We hear it over and over again, "be kind." Our parents tell us this, our schools instruct us to do the same, and society functions on the need for kindness. Why is it that we have such an unkind world? People will say it is just your perspective, and I would agree. Perspective is close to everything in relationships, but the reality is, if you look at the whole of life, people can be very unkind. It is not only in words that kindness fails to show up, it is in the multitude of actions.

I will never dismiss the abundance of kindness that rains on you and me every day! Doesn't kindness make your life and another's so much better? It is perspective to see that, be that, and continue kindness; however, in the deep places of our hearts, we know or have experienced unkindness and further, we know we have been unkind. The great news is that every day people choose kindness for anger, love for hate, and hope for loss. The world is better when someone is kind.

Where does kindness start? If not you, then who? Kindness does not mean you take whatever someone gives you. When you are truly kind, you do not let people push you around, for then you are participating in unkindness by acceptance. It means you think and make something better out of whatever has been given to you. It means you know what kindness looks like, so you will be its hands and heart. It means whatever is done to you, you do what is better for the situation, not what the situation did to you.

## *Everybody can show up; nobody gets it right all the time*

Kindness is found on the high road on the humble way in life. Sometimes that means standing up and calling someone out. Sometimes, it means you messed up and try again. Nobody gets kindness right, all the time, with all people. Kindness may be offered as a re-run after a messy situation, but be careful; the sequel may not be as good as getting the original right.

Being kind has life implications. You don't know what the person next to you is going through; it may be a lot. They may look whole, but the truth is you don't know. I told a lady next to me (who appeared very poised and together) that I hope she was having a good day. She looked at me and started crying, proceeding to tell me she had lost a friend to suicide that week and she couldn't fathom why a man who had so much would let it all go.

I didn't expect that response to a simple expression. I left her, after expressing my sorrow and letting her talk, with the always reminder, "You don't know what someone's life is like unless you are walking in his moccasins." If you are involved with people, you will get these kinds of stories, too. Life can always use your dose of kindness and the frequency of dispensing is never too often.

Unkindness is found on the spectrum of all ages, all genders, cultures, and all races. Sometimes we can just be in a really bad way and we do the unkind thing without a care about what another person is dealing with! I have been here; I have been the unkind one. Hurting people hurt people. When I have hurt someone or they have hurt me, I try to think about that short phrase and understand.

Like poverty, unkindness will never be fully eradicated. You get an assignment every day when your feet hit the floor; will you be kind? You have a lot of people riding on that hope, not just for the moment, but also for the ever-coming minutes to follow. Being kind to the person next to you just might save a life, and that life could be your own.

*"Kindness causes us to learn, and to forget many things."*

*Finish Well*

# Marker 15
# Be Ready to Live, Ready to Die

Those who are most ready to die, are most able to live. Until we have shaken hands with death, we will never walk united with life. It is a paradox it seems, that we accept death to find life, but it is truly so. You are most alive when you can understand death's power comes in living fearlessly and respectfully towards it.

I think the hard part about death is how we will die. No one gets early clues in life about how we will leave this world. Wondering too much or too long is dying little deaths before death. We cannot be prepared for how or when death will come; we can only prepare for death by living well. A well- lived life is good preparation for death. There is a lot of mystery to life and as well, to death. People who have it all figured out, well, they puzzle me. A certain amount of mystery, before God and man, seems to be the best posture for a heart.

## Surrender to live

Surrender offers you the best opportunity for life in its many forms and places, from love to death. A release of one thing brings in another. When you surrender, you are not saying you give up. You are saying you let go of the way you feel life must be and you walk with the way things are, at least for those things you cannot control. Surrender usually comes at the expense of great difficulty and travail. Most of us do not do it willingly, until something asks us firmly.

Walking in agreement with surrender comes from learning to let go and lying down, which comes from wisdom and experience. Sometimes we get this wisdom from observing, but most of the time we have to be close and personal with the lessons life teaches us. That is helpful because we become first-hand learners and the lessons are living to us.

Making peace with the end of your life will make you better to give to where you are in life as you look to the finish line. When you ask yourself what you would do if you only had one more day, you ask yourself the question of what you should be doing today. Death does not stop its ways and times, but when you can make peace with death, you find new freedom to live. When you are not afraid anymore, it is amazing what happens inside of you and to you!

*"The tragedy of life is not that it ends so soon, but that we wait so long to live it."*

# Marker 16
# Run With Wonder

Did you invite yourself into life today? Did you ask the heavens to open for you and give you what you needed today? Did you ask to be surprised with life today? Someone recently told me, older people have lost the wonder of life. That was sad to me and sometimes even young people have lost the wonder. It is really easy to understand that line of thought, if you have lived very long. Life can get burdensome, cumbersome, and wearisome. I have been there. Losing the wonder is losing your direction on the racecourse. It is like running blind; you can't negotiate very well and you surely are not up for anything that will come your way, good or bad.

Look at a child at play. Everything excites him. The dirt goes in the mouth, the rocks, the toys; the fingers are all sources of adventure and joy to him. There are endless things for him to explore and he never seems to tire of exploring. Look at the budding vocabulary and word progression and smiles. When his eyes catch yours watching him doing something, he is so pleased you notice and are engaged. That is wonder. It is refreshment in life. It is the sound of life.

When we have lost the wonder, we need to do some wandering. We need to explain to ourselves why and then we need to honestly ask wonder to come visit us again. We lose so much without wonder in our life. We won't explore, we won't try new things, and we won't stop the world and get off (the train needs to breakdown) to get turned on to life. We don't miss it, sometimes, because we have been lulled to not need it, though we need it badly.

Take away the busy, take away the hurried, take away the hurt, take away the fear, and bring in love with hope and you can find the wonder. Training your mind to look at the sorrows of life differently and training your mind to not take everything so personally and find offense in the slightest remark, reintroduces the possibility of wonder again. Repeating these steps helps you feel your heart sing again. Invite the wonder in along the race of life and you will finish well.

*"Be bold with your dreams. Nurture the dreams that inspire you to go beyond your limits."*

# Marker 17
# Health and Wealth = Friends

Someone recently said to me you only have so much time and health. Well, I think you can add wealth also. So many things we enjoy are "fixed." We know all too well that life is short, even if lived long. We know those who are fine one day and then a change in health or an accident comes and everything changes. Yes, we do know as in the current economic times, wealth is changeable.

Being friends with your health means having a vested interest in it, with what you do know, and doing something good for it! Moderation is the word, not preaching. I may have a formula I think is good and you may have one you think is, but one that is good for both of us is to be moderate. Moderation will save your figure and maybe your life! It asks of us to be reasonable and as a good friend, we should answer back, "I will." You will do more and get more from life with a moderate outlook, not only with health, but also with so many things.

One reason we fail is because we may be people of extremes. Our world is geared up like this by constantly telling us we have failed, so do this, or we must watch for this food or that chemical, etc. We are literally bombed by information that detonates our compass direction in life. Filtering through the maze and haze to find a reasonable and happy way to live is caring for your health. You know what is up here–fresh food, lots of water, exercise, and moderate use of other things. Your health will take care of you now and later.

Your wealth affects your health and your living. I hate to use never, but NEVER be a slave to debt. Do not buy what you can't afford; it takes away your freedom and it hurts other's freedom. Just look at what the home implosion has done to America. Excessive debt may be near thievery if you do not intend to pay it back.

You would not want to work and have someone owe you money and then not pay you back. It is the "doing unto to others" principle that helps one finish well on the race of life. The health race will always find you challenged, but caring for your health will possibly save you from challenges you will not have to face later in life.

*"If I would have known I was going to live this long, I would have taken better care of my health."*

## Marker 18
## Train Your Thoughts, Trust Your Gut

So much of life is lived between two ears. Battles are won and lost in this area less than 12 inches across! No correlation is so great…how you think determines how you feel and live. Most of us desire to be better thinkers. It is not that we can't; it is if we will! Willing requires conscious, repeated, diligent work. Here is the hard work of life, thinking well.

Athletes train long and hard to get to the podium. Training your thoughts takes time, awareness, love (much, much of it), and great resolve with hard work. Shortcuts you will not find in this race, so again, bring patience and the friendship of time with you. It seems simple, but the process of how we think results into the way we interact in our world, both with others and ourselves. We can get many places, many different ways, but the way we think will determine how nice the journey will be.

Thinking well is effort, repeated effort, and sometimes, I don't want to do the work. Thoughts and feelings produce action, even if only in subtle ways. When I am angry with someone and refuse to change my position about him or her, I may think I do not show it or can hide it. Then a day comes when I see that person. I might try to not meet up with him eye to eye or I hold back and act "cool" rather than kind. I still felt mad, my actions "showed" my thinking. I was thinking mad and I acted mad, even subtly; in a sense, my thoughts were with me and my actions showed me so.

## Good thinkers feel and live better

What is the big deal? Everything! This is how we can hurt people and how we hurt ourselves. We may leave poor thinking habits and tendencies unattended and fail to better our thinking. Those behaviors stay with us and they tarnish others both personally and professionally. They destroy communication and goodwill! Relationships lose their edge over time with this unchecked and unresolved way of thinking, then producing actions. We all probably have relationships where we feel something is not right, but have done nothing. Our thinking, as well as the other person's, is one of the main reasons for our distance. Good marriages know and fight this. Without a generous sprinkling of love, we may lose those we wish to love.

Actions, our visible clues, tell us about what we are thinking. If I can let go of thinking that does not profit, and let my charms and generous self work to create right thinking (I am being gracious to myself here, aren't I?), I can face people and situations much better. My thinking and heart are cleaner. I have a good chance of getting a good result in my actions from better thinking. Others run the risk of even having their feelings changed about me! Our lives touch and affect a multitude!

Having "stinking" thinking in life will make you think in foul ways. Sometimes, you many not realize that your thinking is sabotaging your life! The line between what you think and what you do with that thinking will be the outcome of your living. Looking at "Caution Ahead" will offer a view on the big three pitfalls of relating. Thinking is not an "old dog that can't learn new tricks." Thinking can be changed and rearranged, any time, any age. It is just when you and I choose to do it! I think now is a good time.

## Trust your gut

Gut, that word sounds so uncouth for the magic it brings. Do we call it our gut, as in stomach, because that is where one feels instruction or pain as we look for answers to our questions? Intuition sounds like a much nicer word, way more proper. Different words, but essentially the same meaning. We KNOW this. Using the gut's magic is what we may not know or obey.

Trusting your gut can do so much for your life; it might even save it. The mother who throws all reason out and doesn't wait when a doctor has told her to wait, but rushes her very sick infant to the hospital learns time was very critical. The man about to enter a business deal and just doesn't feel something is right, who acts and says, "I'm not able to join you." Your gut is a sixth sense and a true gift.

## Messages from the gut

Paying attention to our gut seems like a choice in our best interest. Why do we so often take so long to learn from it and trust it? We may wonder if it is rational since we cannot quantify it. Gavin DeBecker's book, *The Gift of Fear*, calls the gut an internal guardian that warns you about danger and people. "Listen to it," he says. *New Scientist* calls the gut, "emotions from the unconscious mind that reflect more information than the rational mind." The article stated to trust the rational more than the gut, though, in unfamiliar situations. I guess it takes experience for the gut to offer useful information, a bit like real life!

Our gut instincts play into our life choices. Here was a fun test. When choosing a date (and might it not be a good idea for a marriage partner), pick a person you would pick from a logical sense and then pick one who makes your heart sink. Hands down, the one to pick was the one who made your heart sink, according to a survey on intuition.

We would make far fewer mistakes if we believed and trusted that wisdom, rather than believe it was opposed or harmful to us. Some of the most violent things that happen to us are because we believe something to be true when it is not. We want something to be so, though our gut speaks, we do not listen. Sometimes under better situations the answer could have yielded another word, but it didn't, and we didn't listen.

When your gut nudges you, it is for good reason. That nudge may even show up in a physical sense, probably one reason the word "gut" came into being, because we often feel the emotions of a situation in our stomach. You will have the pleasure of making a lot of decisions in this life. You will never get them all right, but you have resources at your instant call, right inside of you. Operating under intuition's call will save you from heartbreak, health break, and relationship break. Your gut just might be a main voice you should be hearing from, as you travel to finish well on the road of life.

*"You are what you think, not what you think you are."*

*"Let your heart guide you, it whispers, listen closely."*

*Finish Well*

# Marker 19
# Expert Advice Recommended

BE an expert at something you love and enjoy. This is courtesy of my sister. She has told me this for a long time. Going to school, watching someone who is accomplished at their trade, and keeping up on being the best at what you do and enjoy, finds expert next to your name. Hard work transfers into good living. Laziness and idleness bring forth disappointment, both externally and within. Yes, hard work is in the recipe here, but it is work that really brings you something and takes you somewhere. There are no shortcuts, so do not ask for them.

Being the best you can be in your work, your family and your personal life will repay you in happy ways. As my manager would tell us, "Who would want to be just average? I want to be the best I can be at my job." I believe we all have a desire to master something. Paying good attention to what brings you pleasure or what you have natural ability for is a signal for what you might be an expert in. Someone needs the expert you are or can become!

## Enjoy a good read

One way to be an expert is to read! There must be thousands of books, magazines, and different reading materials in our world. Information overload it seems at times—from the computer to print media—overwhelms us. A good read raises the enjoyment of life and grows an expert. I was not a good reader growing up, but I love it now. Today, I cannot get enough reading. I continue to profit from reading every day.

Reading creates, inspires, and continues to keep you in the school of learning. An expert lives and grows in the school of learning. You will get old very fast when you stop learning. Every day is a new adventure when you read. How I treasure knowing something today that I did not yesterday. I have a few books by my bed that are my good night buddies. I try to never go to bed without saying goodnight to them by reading from them. They wind me down after a busy day and put my mind in a wonderful posture for sleep. They, sometimes, even inspire and excite me to anticipate and welcome another day.

Reading is important because it helps create an intentional and instructed life. It is almost like having a coach beside you to instruct you in wisdom and joy. Reading's other gift is the offering and filling of the present moment. Though reading can help you dream, it brings everything enjoyed to the moment. Life is just that much better when you have a moment and you are redeeming the minutes.

## Who, me? An expert?

What makes someone "better" than you is what he or she has become an expert in. Now, it does not make them better to boast, but better to serve. If I can command people in a correct way, I must do that to lead and serve. If I can hit a golf ball beautifully (pure, as sweet son would say) and score well, I must use that wonder and awe someone has of me, to give as well as enjoy. Much given, much required.

If you are an expert, no one should force you to use your skills, but everyone is better for the use of your talents and skills. You may be "better" than me in the skill you do, with the skill you have. You might sew better than I do, maybe you hem better, or the seams you finish are nicer. Whatever it is, when you compare (and believe me, you better be a comparer in life) some things are better, and being an expert is where the better is.

We know some things are subject to subjectivity and comparison, like test scores, beauty contests, horse shows, a famous music show, etc. What does it matter for the expert? How can we decide who is an expert and who is not or is it worth being one? Is it worth being in the competitive world of "experts?"

Life offers no easy black and whites here, does it? It still offers you plenty of reasons to pursue excellence and strive to be an expert. You keep trying. You keep learning. You keep doing. You say no to giving up. Maybe your ship has not come in, but it will. Just be sure you have not passed on too many ships or let fear stop you from boarding.

Experts are in demand. Experts have an opportunity to live a purposeful life and do much good. Purpose brings joy. Experts use their knowledge with the ways of perseverance to do something better than could be left undone. Creating your life around something you love to do and then doing all you can to create that life is a wonderful way to live and an even more wonderful way to finish well.

*"We give advice by the bucket, but take it by the grain."*

# Marker 20
# My Success is Not Your Success

I love a game when there is a winner and I am that winner! Winning and being first is such fun. What I really enjoy is a game that everyone can play and still win, that is life! What I even enjoy more about that game is you get to decide how you can win at that game. Success is important to everyone; it is just defined differently for each of us. Your definition of success will be different at different ages and seasons in your life.

That definition may be similar to one you had as a youth, but just keeps evolving. For some, success is having five children, a wonderful marriage, and living in the country. Can I disagree? Others want to run a company, lead others, and make a large salary. Can I disagree?

The joy of reading this page is you get to define success your way. The challenge is to define success after a time of thought, reflection, and insight. This topic is useful in wonderful conversation under a tree, with ample time, and with someone you value. Defining success relationally and contributorily has always served me well.

Meaningful interaction with those who you care most about and who care about you is about as good as it gets. Anything else is gravy, as we use to say growing up! Relationships always offer longer rewards than a goal or money. They are much harder to come by, but they are worth it. Your money or status will never tell you they love you!

A life that merely takes, is a life taken from the joy of serving others. Being useful, beyond what pleases you, can be great pleasure for both you and the one you please. When you are full, you have so much to give and someone can use that giving. Striving to live a full life with the characteristics of a good finisher can create the opportunity to spill over into other's lives. It doesn't take long to think who has spilled into your life. It's a good exercise of encouragement to think about who has added to your life.

Giving, freely, your time, your energy, and your enthusiasm to individuals and organizations brings life to you and to those who get you! There are so many good causes that need your influence, not merely your money.

A man probably views success differently than a woman, but that just fits into what success is — your definition. I know many who view a successful life as one that serves God and man. When you find your definition, what follows will be the energy you put into to your life's mission!

*"Act as if what you do makes a difference. It does."*

# Marker 21
# Bad Day, or Is It?

I think there are such things as bad days, don't you? It's easy to say "bad dog" to the misbehaving dog who just ate the couch. It is not so easy to say "bad day" when you are taught you shouldn't feel that way and be grateful instead. Some days are just not very nice days to you and me...or so we think. Perhaps, that bad day was doing something good for your "another" day.

She is a beautiful, vivacious 40-something who lost her husband when I lost hope. He was dying, while I was dying in another way. Her five children are amazingly kind and loving, a tribute to her and her loving relationship with her husband. Their bad day kept on, but so did she. Today, you would notice not a hint of wear, unless you spoke to her about the pain. She has gone forth to create her fill of good days.

The story doesn't end. She has met another man, a widower with five kids, both of them sharing the same day and year anniversary. They are engaged. That good day did come, even after dark clouds! Oh, the story is not over, but the lesson is... Was that bad day for her and her children really a bad day?

Oh, it was a day they will never forget and never wish happened. I think it is very reasonable to call it a bad day. It was also a day they could hardly believe would ever bring another one, another good day. The friendship of time has brought her so much joy and hope, though now coupled with a soberness and greater joy of life. She is amazed what time has brought her personally, and for the joy of seeing a good day.

## Something good about a bad day

This is not to say there are no "bad" days; we will have "bad" days, but that is only part of the story about them, too. Lessons from bad days come from those who have kept on the road, only to see bad days do yield to good days. There is always something good about a bad day. Maybe it comes to make you appreciate something you should have before, or maybe you vowed you would do something differently after one or maybe you asked a question of yourself you needed to ask.

This is what life is for, appreciating, vowing, and answering. It sounds great to have an easy life, but have you ever thought about it? An easy life would be a hard life. You would be untrained to face what you must face to be strong. Life would actually be harder, and you, less filled with depth and grace. You would lose out and so would the world that is waiting for your wisdom and strength.

There are a lot of beautiful people in the world and some of them have come up the hard and difficult way.

## Bad Day, or Is It?

Not by their making alone, you may not choose all your burdens, though you may answer how you will carry them. One thing you can choose is how you will look at a bad day.

*"The more sand that has escaped from the hour glass, the clearer we should see through it."*

*Finish Well*

# Marker 22
# Run Clean

You will sleep so much better following this marker. As a young man told me, living an honest life will have you not be sad at the end. We often think we will get further from cheating. We will get something, maybe no one will know how we did it, and then we get it and it forever twinges in our heart when we remember. The conscience is like that. A good conscience is a good help on the way to finishing well. It is essential, unless your conscience is seared or overly guilty.

Run clean first with you, you cannot silence all who accuse; even sometimes you can't silence your inner critic. Here is where your thinking is so critical. Aim for the high side of your beliefs. Not feverish pressure, but strong resolve to be and make peace with what you can and with what you can't, way easier said then done. Then find ways to run clean with others. How? Find a way that means something to you and the other person; humility always runs well. Strive to be a good competitor in life by living honorably.

When you fail, admit it; do the repair work. It is easier than being continually wounded. Getting back on course should not be so difficult and we should make this available to those who have not run clean but are trying to. Wouldn't you like someone to understand your heart and your intentions that are trying to work for peace and connection? Our pride and spirit are on the line at times like this and it would be so nice for someone to accept you without a legal form of DOs.

## Guilt and fairness

The number of troubled consciences could go way down and you could be a great forgiver. Everyone looks at matters differently. Some feel extreme guilt for minor things, others little for major ones. Being wounded when you offer an olive branch is very hard. Being so exact with an apology is exasperating and defeating.

A man is demoralized when he must repeat he is sorry ten times when, though he doesn't apologize like a woman wants, he has said he is sorry, and probably feels very deeply about wronging her. I have been a slow learner here, because of stupid things I read on apologies and also feeling I needed to do it and have it done right. I lost a lot of good will from this.

Be fair. Oh, and that too, again is variable between the sexes and others. What is fair? "The only fair I know of is the Pomona Fair," said the lady on the airplane next to me. That is probably about as good a definition of fair as I can think of. Nevertheless, strive to a high level of fairness that pulls you to better thoughts and doings. You won't hit

## Run Clean

it and neither will the other person, but that doesn't mean give up; it means, it is so worth fighting for.

Don't get ahead on a false premise. What is it worth? Every place you stand needs to be firm. Firm from living truthfully. Firm from thinking and doing the best, firm from living the higher road, and firm from taking no short cuts when you need to climb up the long and hard way. You might get something when you do things the other way and one thing you will get is sorrow. The heart understands and keeps check of things not agreeable and honest with others and us. It is so not worth it when we attempt to secure something from dishonesty. We are not immune to the pressure that dishonesty asks of us. No, it pesters us and comes again and again to ask us to take its way. Let this be a warning, when your heart repeatedly senses something you do not have peace with, do not go forward. It seems a good thing and holds promise for you in the future, or so you think, but you may be very sorry in the days ahead. Maybe it does have the potential for promise under different circumstances or at another time, but do it the right way, so you can enjoy it all the way.

You won't be perfect on the race. Who is or will be? You will fail to live up to your standards, you will do something you so wished you never did, and you will wish you could change an outcome, but you can't. Redeem the time and give yourself time to mourn the mistake, and then give yourself the mistake to learn from and try to never go there again.

*"The journey is the reward." — Chinese proverb*

*Finish Well*

# Marker 23
# Make Love to Life

When a runner crosses the finish line, so much goes through his mind, but one thing especially; I did it, success achieved! After the race, it is not unusual for a runner to study his race and think about what happened, the good and bad strategies, what went right, and what went wrong.

A runner knows what the race means to him. Finishing may get you a medal or certificate, but why and how you run the race expresses your PASSION. If the race of life is meant merely to endure it, then I can't think of a more miserable way to live. If just getting through is your goal and mine, I pity us both. We have missed the ride.

Passion is always in fashion, as music groups, horses, nightclubs, and a woman's football organization attach their name to it. Passion walked into essence in music and poetry in the Romantic period when the theme was "passion over reason." Forever debated is the concept, but I like Antonio Damasio's thought, "Feelings can cause havoc, but their absence can be no less damaging." Passion, an indispensable feeling and value, creates and sustains life. It is just that good.

A young girl who set out on her quest to hike overseas is missing. She has been featured in print and television. Her family desperately wants to find her, but she is missing. Her motto on her website is "Make love to life." At first, I thought it too sexual to have as a motto, but then I got to know what she was all about, and I saw passion.

## Passion is never far from the one seeking it

Passion is the fire that lights up the soul and makes it do something it cannot stop doing or feeling—that something is the fire of passion! Every day I see passion —someone's or mine. Passion sends lovers out to exotic places or in the sharing of simple meaningful words or gestures. Passion creates new life in the birth of babies and ideas. Passion compels you up and carries you further than you could ever go without having it! Passion is somewhere near you every day and life is better for it. Not just better for it, your life is created for its expressions. Nothing great and good happens without passion. Passion is movement; apathy is still.

When we have lost the fire of passion for life and what we are and can do, we are as the smoldering coals over a fire, nearly out. Waking up your heart is the beginning place, after you have been asleep too long. When passion is low, I stir the coals of the fire and see where and how they can be ignited again. Some days require more work than others and some days, like someone said to me, "You're on fire!"

What if everyone "made love to life?" I sure see a lot of people "make fear to life" and "make hate to life." I even see wonderful people make "caution to life." There is a time for caution. Withholding the use of your life and its gifts are not a time for caution. They are given to you for appreciating, sharpening, and using. They are for time to be loud, though they may serve quietly.

Reading stories of passion and seeing its power without a cord inspire! Your life is just plain amazing. Have you ever thought of it like that? Imagine now, how much better your life is for passion — what you have and what keeps you going — passion plays in it. And then, look at passion that has gone out or gone afraid. There is always something or someone looking to take our passion away, just don't let it be you!

*"Love in its essence is spiritual fire."*

*Finish Well*

# Marker 24
# Marry Your Best Friend

Best friends are one of the "bests" life has to offer. A best friend will keep you in life a lot longer and stronger. The ties that bind are never tighter than with someone you deeply love and do life with. I have "a generous handful" of wonderful friends. In fact, at this time in my life, I have recognized one important thing — know who your true friends are — know who is really in your "camp."

Relationships are the foundations of anything good you and I will have in life. You can never go it alone here. That doesn't mean at all you must be married. It means you must be in good relationships. Your health and much of your personal wellbeing are related to the quality of relationships you have. A poor relationship affects more than your attitude; your health is at risk.

As we age, most of us were once filled with so much hope and promise. Then what happens amazes us; we lose the wonder of life and discovery. People tell us that it is the way it is supposed to be. I will buy that a little, but even with all the hard parts of life, there are mountains to climb and those mountains are to explore! If you are not better for the journey, you have missed something, whether married or single.

## Along for the journey

Having someone along that journey makes it so much better. That someone can be a friend or lover and I hope you have a nucleus of true ones, if only a few. The one best friend I hope you get is the one you marry. It may seem silly to say that, but I ask this question of people and I asked this recently of one married 63 years. "Why has your marriage lasted?" This is what she said, "Marry your best friend."

"Doesn't everyone marry their best friend?" would be the reply? No, they don't. As a friend once told me, we often marry the dream. We marry the idea of having children, the nice house, and the station and status in life and love we so long for. We may marry what our parents or our community asked of us, or worse, when we think we have to get married because we have reached a certain age. We may marry to please instead of being pleased with the beloved and the beloved pleased with us.

We do not get everything right in life, and some choices we make do not turn out quite as we had wished. Who you marry is such a significant decision, your hope and self-concept are wrapped up in how and who you love. Waiting to get married until you know what you want in a mate and what you will give to a mate is a good wait. That proposition takes time and honesty.

## Never forget your heart in decisions

Marry from your heart (you must listen to it because it will knock again and again, read trail marker #18), not merely your head. All our lives we are taught to be so practical and calculating, as though marriage is a formula, while our hearts speak and we must listen. I am convinced the reason so many marriages are not on good ground is because the people approaching them have never known who they are first, and secondly, who really cares for them. A best friend stands with you through time.

Knowing who you are and what you like takes time. We often do not like the friendship of time — we are in such a hurry. I know people who have set an age deadline for the time to get married. Can I say recipe for disaster? It was. So many other things factor in…unplanned pregnancy (one reason I ask my kids to wait), loneliness, insecurity (feeling no one will love you and now is the chance, as one woman said to me), and desire (we get this one).

We are often too young and dumb (sorry) to listen to our hearts, their warnings and their needs, and impulse is an attribute of an untrained mind and heart. Listening to your heart requires a form of suffering before a victory of triumph. We usually get it throughout the journey, but sometimes we pay dearly for its lesson. Finding a soulmate partner is not impossible, it is not luck; it is wise preparing and planning…and making time a friend, while being your own.

## Good chemistry in the mix

Good chemistry is good science. So what is good chemistry? In the arena of love, some even call it finding his or her soulmate; someone you connect and mix with well.

A soulmate opens the channel where life can run to every corner of a soul and be perfectly content to have touched every place and still find acceptance and love. In those places that are compatible and beautiful to each, there is delight. Those places that are thorny or difficult, there is the ointment of love applied daily and often.

Soulmates make life more beautiful, more creative, and more inspiring. Yes, enjoy the station of your life in singleness and make everything out of that life. Singleness is a gift in its own right. A true soulmate and best friend will make life far richer. A soulmate experience is often captured as lover to lover. The experience of connection can also be found woman-to-woman and man-to-man, even in the bond of parent-to-child or an adult and mentor, as deep sharing is contained in these relationships. Such a glorious thing is love; it seeps into every corner of the soul and no one is poorer for it.

It is not that a relationship does not have soulmate potential; it is much of what we chose to do in our loving. People can have amazing chemistry (they both agreed) but their relationship faltered due to taking one for granted, neglect, misunderstanding, abuse, or addictions. Good care is essential for good chemistry. Taking care of a best friend (make sure you find the first best friend — you), when you have found them or they have found you, is just like caring for a beautiful garden that needs weeding and feeding to remain vibrant and alive. When the care doesn't happen, other things than love grow.

## Emotional divorce

When you are best friends in marriage, there are places you have gone in one another's soul that emotionally divorced and unconnected married partners may never know. Emotional divorce will never have statistics, but so many married people are here. Here people live together and arrive in appearances, but they live a shell of a life. Sometimes, many things have happened that leave them unconnected and uninterested in the other's emotional/ soul wellbeing (that is what emotional divorce really is). Married with no intimacy but married with no true heart and soul connection they find their lives.

Reasons abound for why they are here, often failing to use some of the trail markers presented in *Finish Well* or their own markers. For those in an emotional divorce, it can be one of the loneliest places; obligation overrides the joy of sharing a real life together. Getting out of this place is not easy, especially when the heart has died so much to the relationship. One begins with honesty — the first place of change and healing. Then WHERE you look, either up, out, or in, directs your progress. When you recognize this place, it is a call to be wise and address the situation; doing nothing can make the relationship (and your heart) suffer and die further. The friendship of working with time and the process of change offers you the opportunity to move you and the relationship to a better place.

The countenance on that 63-year-married woman's face was amazing as she said, "I married my best friend." If I could give any gift to a young person or a wishful one, this would be one of them...be patient with the process of love...be true to who you are with another...and listen to your heart, for it has many clues for you to find the WHO or soulmate in your life.

Then when you have, work with love, yes, work with love. Love needs care; we are human, very human. We will fail, even those we are deeply tied to in soul; yet love is worth all it is reported to be and even then some. No one can finish well without love and no one can tell you the exact definition of love. It is constantly enlarging, just as your heart and soul would be. This one is especially for you, my sons. I want you to find how rich you can be with love.

*"Every time I hold you I begin to understand, that everything about you tells me you're my best friend."*

# Marker 25
# Don't Sell Anything

A president of a company told his salesman a distinct piece of advice, just as he was about to leave on a trip. This salesman was required to sell his company's products and he knew doing so would result in a living, if things went well. "Salesmen always sell" was his reasoning. The company president proceeded to leave him with a final word upon his departure. Waiting for the word, the young salesman could not wait to hear the wisdom of the president's advice. He was ready for something earth-shaking to take on his trip.

The president left him with these words, "Don't sell anything." Wow, this was not the advice he thought the president would tell him as he was about to leave. He was too young and embarrassed to ask what he meant and spent days thinking about what the president said. In time he finally got it! What is it that he understood?

The salesman came to understand that you know your product, believe in your product, and share information about your product, but it will do the selling (a good product will show its value) when you don't force the product on someone.

## Don't make a hard sell

This is a truth for life. Don't sell anybody anything that is making him or her endure a hard sell or a have to sell. Even great salesmen know a great product is the best salesman and they are merely facilitators. No matter what you do in life, pressure is no fun on either side. Okay, the real world may have a lot of it, but you don't have to be in the channel, at least not for all you do. That means, let your kids learn some things without pounding in information and let them have the pleasure of seeing how they will bring in that lesson, on their own, because they need the information or "that product."

Letting others have the joy of "getting" something or sharing what they have learned is much more fun (but it requires patience) than the constant nagging that could be done to instill information. Even if you know much, teach it quietly, allowing others the comfort of coming to you for information. If you have knowledge and wisdom, it is good to share, but how you share makes all the difference in the world.

If the sharing of information makes someone feel bad or burdened, maybe another way to do it needs to happen. No one in a sense likes to be told, especially all the time. Sometimes, it is really not a kid's fault they do not get something quickly; it is just the process of learning we are impatient to. This is where time is a parent's good friend, when used properly, time and loving instruction.

Business and personal information manuals tell you to sell yourself, and in a sense, we do that the minute we walk through a door. You do not need to sell yourself in the sense of a hard sell. We are always growing and learning. Does that mean we are inadequate when we are not at a certain point in someone's process or guidebook? I have seen too many beaten down kids and people to realize too much is expected of others, by others, who would probably want compassion and do things much similarly if they had the same situation.

## Respect and truth

Self-respect and respect for where you are at in your life creates the best opportunity for you to finish well. You must not run someone's race with his or her expectations; you will merely just perform and check your heart. Someone who takes a different way to learn or amount of time is not deficient; they are working with what they have. Let the quality of your life sell for you and rest in who that person is, not trying to be who you are not. "True North, True You" is a look at this thought.

When you understand the product you have, appreciate it, and grow confidently. Your ship will come in and it will sail beautifully. Force anyone to do something, even you, and you get stress, resistance, and pressure. There is a better way to live and enjoy life, a better way to finish well.

"Unity in things necessary. Liberty in things doubtful. Charity in everything."

# Marker 26
# Details and Small Things, Please

A good manager must pay attention to details. Missing a piece in the workplace puzzle could alter a forecast, cost millions, or place someone in a job that is not comfortable. A person who wants to finish well loves details. He or she is not obsessed with them, but values them. A husband knows that remembering a wedding anniversary may be no small thing to a wife. A wife knows that a clean and pressed shirt in the closet means "I love you" to a man. Little ways we care about others, especially those in our inner circle, will affect our ride to finish well.

Remember what is important to your lover. If he or she is excited about it, then remember it. If she loves a certain perfume, chocolate, or activity, put it on your agenda and better yet, write it on your heart, so you will never forget! If he loves the San Francisco Giants and a couch on Sunday, make it an honor for him to have the moments. Husbands or boyfriends, think of what she loves and needs, even ask her! Wives or girlfriends, prepare your life for some fun, doing things he loves.

Loving what others love and paying attention to what they love are living indicators of how you love. It's not just, tell me, it's show me. You show others how you care about them in the details and small things. It really isn't very hard, but it requires your attention. People who value others will pay attention.

Never underestimate the power of small things. That includes the small quiet voice of your child or spouse from their spirit, a word or gentle touch, or the joy of another day doing what you love with those you love. It is easy to be lulled by the constant noise of life and "tyranny of the urgent" but do not listen and obey their calls. You are on your way to the finish line when you have loved and learned what it means to pay attention to details and small things.

*"Maintaining a complicated life is a great way to avoid changing it."*

# Marker 27
# Shoulder a Burden

It is no secret; we all have secrets. We all have burdens, past and present. If we could peer inside another, we would be surprised how many burdens others carry. If we would be open and honest, we would be similarly surprised how many we have. Thinking well and being positive is great, but so is sharing a burden, yours and someone else's.

Some burdens are easier to carry than others. All burdens are not equal. A friend needs a shoulder before a judge. You can never fully understand your own pain, much less another's. It is best, therefore, to have strong shoulders and let others lean on them. You will need someone's strong shoulder someday, if you haven't rested on one yet.

## Suffer a burden

The great quote, "Suffering may be mandatory, but misery is optional," is certainly true. Sometimes, though, we are not at that place, though we are trying to find a place void of misery. Good friends won't leave you in the place of misery, but also won't punish you for being there. Few come out of struggles without first being in places they do not wish they were found in.

Sometimes people carry burdens by default. Many times I have seen someone do something kind, only to be subject to misunderstanding or injury. I have seen people offer loving help and have their kind gestures and funds taken. I have seen people give assistance, only to be wrongly accused. Here, only God knows the situation and one must suffer the burden and let time either solve it or bring comfort. This is the place of real work in one's soul, when one has done no wrong, but is charged with it. I venture to say, this is more common than ever spoken.

A family released a huge amount of debt owed to another family in their partnership after it was dissolved. They struggled because the amount was quite large and they felt wronged, but they also realized the holding of anger and loss of this money would not make the other party change or make payment. They decided they could use the "gesture of tomorrow" in forgiveness and they would go on with that decision. This was not an easy decision, but they choose to suffer a burden and then satisfy it with forgiveness.

## Satisfy a burden

Finally, make a burden work for you; satisfy it. I have a friend who was unable to bear children. It broke her heart. She decided to love others children through her work. She got "her children" and she found an outlet for children and a burden satisfied.

The burden of a grudge or an error that brings unchangeable moments, can they work for you? A woman once told an audience her teacher disliked her so much and would not pass her in a program. She did all she was told to do and had good work behavior, but the subjective evaluation from the teacher said, "fail." It broke her heart to not graduate with her class, but she went another semester, with another instructor, and passed. She referenced how much work happened in her soul from that terrible time and she has seen the burden work for her in life, even years later.

You have your burdens and I have mine. Whether you shoulder, suffer, or satisfy them, what you do with them makes all the difference in the world!

*"Kindness, more than deeds, is an attitude, an expression, a look, a touch. It is anything that lifts another person."*

*Finish Well*

# Marker 28
# Go Away

Dad always taught me the value of a vacation or going away. It was never optional in my family; it was something you just did. Being from a military family made travel the norm for me. I didn't appreciate it then, like I do now. That seems to happen with a few years on you. You look at things a lot differently. So, please go away for a while, see different sights, and do things you wouldn't do while you are at home.

A CNN health story in May 2011 reported how good a vacation is and how seeing different things is good for the brain, especially seeing other cultures. We knew that, nobody had to make it official. That is why it is nice to drive home a different way or make a break in the roll and routine of life. Monotony needs an adjustment from time to time. One thing I notice about people who are older is they crave routine, sometimes too much. Being flexible, doing things differently, and trying new routines bring lessons and life to you. Those things can even bring excitement to you.

Never more than now do I feel people need to go away. There is always so much to do at your place of business, where you volunteer, what you do at home, etc. There will always be so much to do. I look at my hands and marvel how much work has come forth from them, from birth to raising a family to now. I am only one set of hands; yours have done so much as well. I continue to be amazed at what others do. We need to go away. Our lives are counting on it. They have more to give us and going away is one way we get more from them.

## Don't let money keep you from going away

Vacations cost money, but money must never be the focus of everything you and I do (granted, easier said than done). Some of the best things in life are free, anyway. I love to hike and I do that for free where I live. I also spend money to travel to hike for free! Outside has never lost the allure for me; there are too many sunsets yet to see and photograph. There are too many smiles, laughs and hugs to share with those you love in removed places where you can just "chill." Going away, going somewhere, sometime, is an ingredient in the finish well equation.

Some of the best ways you can spend your money is to see new places and cultures. Even here in the United States we have different cultures in different states, in a sense. Dad always told me, though he had travelled the world, that we have a varied and exciting country to see and visit right here. Whatever it takes to go somewhere,

## Go Away

find a way to go. You get to do the choosing, you get to do the savoring. The best option is to go away.

Your mind, your body, and your relationships will be better for going away. The change in routine and escape from the every day are so welcomed, most any time, in life. Settle for some things, but not for going away moments, that add and build you a life you want to live.

*"A ship is safe in the port, but that is not what a ship is for."*

*Finish Well*

# Marker 29
# Celebrate Moments

Is it not safe to say we love celebration? One can make anything a celebration out of anything to celebrate. It is not just the celebrations on a calendar you celebrate; it is the steps you make and awaken to in life that create celebration. Those steps are individual, sometimes, and those steps are worth marking. Nothing gives pleasure like the anticipation of an event. Anticipation is not overrated. It pulls you through some tough times and keeps you travelling with hope.

Remember when the school dance was a month away and you were out shopping for the dress? What about the new position you got at work that put you in a new office space? That special toast with a special someone or group is forever etched in your mind. The place, the smell, the season make for a lasting memory and spectacle of goodwill with who is sharing these moments with you. I can still get a whiff of a scent of certain men's cologne and I find myself light-years' away from today.

## Moments are your creations

Your moments mean the entire world to you, and rightly they should. Finding the time to let moments live in your life and those you love, connect you with them. If you do not, you miss the show of life and the inner connection of celebratory moments. The joy of these moments is they are often at your will and command. You master and engineer those moments as you plan for them. They are your creations.

Let nothing stop you from meeting with those minutes of life because one day those minutes are no more. We cannot imagine this place at certain periods in our life. In fact, it is easy to live thinking we will always have what we have at the present, which is so far from the truth. We come to know this in fuller measure as we age. You really do have this moment, your best moment, in the sense you may not have another.

Celebrate difficult moments, too, not in the sense of being happy to have them, but in being useful to share them with those who need you. A funeral is not a moment we love to embrace, but we need to share and be there many times more than we wished to attend. Moments tell others you are showing up for their life, the joys and the sorrows. If you care, you will care to show up. Sure, there will be difficult times, but make them very few and always strive to choose well. It may make all the difference as you seek to finish well.

*Celebrate Moments*

"Life is not measured by the number of breaths we take, but by the moments that take our breath away."

*Finish Well*

# Marker 30
# Race With All Ages

You will meet many people on the road of life, some younger and some older and some your age. A friend once told me you need three types of people on your journey. She told me, "Have someone younger to tell them what you have learned, the same age to share with you where you both have been, and someone older who you can pass on wisdom and advice to you." You can be one of these types of people to someone. These kinds of people show up in every place of life, even as strangers.

Having people of all ages in your life is usually easy. This often happens naturally in life, but some places buck the process. They have reasons for doing this; I just like some things about the natural process of life with people at various ages. Seeing this natural process work quite well has made me have this viewpoint. One thing I did not like about the organized educational system is grouping kids in the same age group for most of the day, most of the year. Okay, I probably could get a hundred, "I don't like," on that one, but hear my reasoning.

Where else in real life does this age grouping happen naturally? A home, a workplace, workout studios, and houses of worship have all varying ages. We learn most from those who have gone before us who teach us and we get the opportunity and pleasure to influence those younger than us by example and instruction. Even younger people can be teachers. My children taught me more than I could have ever taught myself alone! I love watching the senior in high school help the toddler bounce a basketball and I love seeing the large eyes of the young boy looking up to the talented football player.

Those our own age can be good buddies to us. We have had a lot of similar life experiences, visions, and views created around a similar point in time. Sometimes we may be too focused and immature, together, to enhance another's life for major growing, if we only had these kinds of people in our life. We sometimes compete, criticize, and allow jealousy to reign with those our own age, more than we do when we are older and with various ages. These attitudes seem to change in ways as we age, but the growing years can be especially brutal for those in the same age range. We may view life so narrowly, if we live and laugh, with only those on our age block.

## Strangers on our Way

Strangers touch me all the time. I wonder, are we really strangers when we care? I will never forget Carlton, a man my age, who wondered if I was an angel because he prayed for something to happen in his life one fall morning. I only talked to this bus driver from my heart, but somehow, his heart was ready for mine. I remember the young man who quickly came from behind my car to offer assistance after a major tire shred on an Arizona highway late one night. Though I was afraid being alone on a dark desert highway, a stranger performed love on my car and me. Strangers are wonderful kinds of people in places you may least expect.

I am so thankful for every person, older and wiser, and for every simple and fresh young person with their new or old ideas, words, hope, and outlook. I learn from them. I learn from others my age as we converse about similar things since we are the same age, but the pure joy of recognizing each other's differences and sharing them creates a life better lived. The stranger will always be more than someone I just don't know.

If you want to be and live better, be with those of all ages. Trying to find someone older and wiser who will be involved in your life brings you lessons and wisdom. Being involved with someone who is younger, where you can encourage and teach along the way, offers new looks at old things. You will see that to finish well, you do better by finishing with all ages.

*"If the very old will remember, the very young will listen."*

*Finish Well*

# Marker 31
# Time to BE First

As children we are so often taught to never be first. It was implied that the "first" people are selfish — don't be first in line or first to take that piece of pie. Well, being first here is desirable, not debatable.

BE the first to offer a kind word; you may change an outcome. Never be stingy with your words of kindness. Find people and places to use these "goodness givers" as often as you can, sincerely.

BE the first to smile at someone — even a stranger. Life is softened with smiles and words. People with smiles go further, research says they look better, and smiling is good for your face value! When you ever have a difficult situation, remember to find a smile, it has the power to change a problem! Even better, share your humor and laughter. It is no secret; laughter is great medicine.

BE the first to forgive. If this first has not played out in your life, I am very sad for you. Forgiving keeps you in the game of life and keeps someone else. Oh, so much harder than the written thought. I have been hurt and so have you. I think you hurt me more and I know you feel the same. Unless someone offers the "gesture of tomorrow" in forgiveness, there will be none. Lots of good people get tossed in the sea of unforgiveness, as someone just won't budge from pain or stance. BE the first here, BE the first.

BE the first to be fair, a really hard one, as fair means different things to different people. Trust your "best" self on this one and do look at another's point of view as you decide. If you can't let go of being "fair" on your terms, then BE kind. Part of life's joy is accepting another view without destroying the core value and thoughts of another. We need this return to society in mammoth ways, BE that person. Good relations see WINNING is when both sides come out with something good after an exchange, especially when a little movement can make all the difference in the world.

BE the first to respect and value who you are. So many ideas will swirl in your head and people will make you think they are superior in thought, word, and deed, leading to insecurity of who you are, if you let it. Don't make life a contest, but be true to you and the care of you. This is a lesson that never gets old; you will learn this as the days add to years. Secure it now and be the best friend, to you, that you would ever want or need. Better yet, you will have people who respect and value you.

BE the first to send a personal note when someone has met with you, given you something, or just because they touched you. Oh, yes, there is email, but its letter is nothing like a good old-fashioned one in a box — a mailbox. Be timely in sending it. People never tire of being thought of and neither do you!

BE the best you can be to others. Dad taught me this when he was selling his VW bug in Colorado when I was a teen. I told him he should sell his car for a lot of money because it was a great car and he could get more for it than he asked. He said, "You don't have to make a big profit on something you have had good use on. Let someone else get pleasure from it!" Thank you, Dad. I have never forgotten that lesson; it is fresh in my memory. Find joy in giving something that really costs you money or time — or better yet, love. It may be hard, but it will be satisfying long after you have given.

BEing the first is a good thing. Expand your way of viewing things and BE the first to cheer your fellow runner on the road to finish well.

*"Take nothing but pictures, leave nothing but footprints."*

*Finish Well*

# Marker 32
# Create a Legacy

At times we all like noise. A great concert or the roar of a victory heralds the chance to make it loud! Sometimes, though, it is quiet, that will best do. Just sometimes, the greatest strides are made quietly. The strides of a legacy are made when no one may even notice or hear them.

Legacy takes place in the days-in and days-out of goodwill in a family, friendship or business and community environment. The time and time again of showing up for life and for the people in your life who you and they are forever made better by it. The rhythm and rhyme of life creates legacy portraits, even when you may not know you are photographing or drawing them. Humbling work are the workings of life in creating a legacy.

In quiet places, a mother and father's love and instruction (or sadly, a lack of it) take shape to last a lifetime. Some wounds last when love is hidden or lacking. It's not the perfect these people bring to the whole; it's the giving of a life carried out by love and thoughtfulness. Loving demonstration and thoughtfulness in deed seem to do legacy's work fine.

How you ask? You create a legacy, quietly, by living your values and loving the people who are given to you, family and friends. If you value love, you will attend to what looks like love, and especially, show it. Ask the person you want to bestow your legacy on what love looks like? Watch what makes their eyes light up and smile come. Maybe it is when you cook their favorite meal, teach them how to make it, or go to the special place you both so enjoy go. Maybe it is the fishing trip you take, the baseball game you watch together, or special cabin you go to ski in winter. This is between you and them, and no one else. It is not subject to judgment by any one, at least it is best not.

## *Pictures and possessions and a thousand words*

Photographs are one such way to "legacize" life. Today, it is easier than ever with a computer and keepsake books. Recording family history is another way to secure what has happened is not forgotten. Even the crude writing of notes or more commonly known way, journaling, is a way to keep the legacy going. I have many scribbled notes about my family and the past. Though not fully put together, it does something inside of me every time I see whom these people are, that are a part of who I am.

Keeping a list and place for special items passed down from generation to generation, will be helpful for those who come after you. You will forget the special jewelry or plate your aunt had years down the road, unless you are given to telling and writing. Sometimes, you may feel no one cares except you. That is not important now. If you do, that is what matters. They may later, but you first create a life worth remembering and telling.

How I wish I did not have to believe someone had to be on board with what I thought was good to do. It is so much better to quietly enjoy and do what you love and value for your family or you. Approval is not needed. Time is one piece of legacy's puzzle and we are all not on the same time line. You are probably not trying to find out all about your family history at 20, it usually interests you much later where you do something about it.

One lovely way legacy is quietly lived out is in the passing on of values you value and share. Those gems shared between family members and friends show up on some stage of someone's life, somewhere. They show up when you are not trying so hard, but just caring. You cannot know when the show will be on visible display, but you can be sure creating a legacy takes place when you may least know you are creating and seeing one. Finishers on the race of life know that the fastest may not always be the winner (as in the tortoise and the hare), as well as the loudest runner may not make the greatest mark on the road called legacy. Quiet gets the job done in ways that loud cannot.

*"You must never miss the opportunity to tell the people in your life how much they mean to you."*

*Finish Well*

# AFTER THE RACE — A RUNNER'S REFLECTION

# Experience It All...
# A Blessing From Your Senses

Your world comes to you in the five senses. A sixth sense, call it you're your gut or intuition, joins these five. Enjoying and experiencing life starts and stays here. Who can say which sense is better or most needed? In asking the question, you will find it is most difficult to choose which one you could live without. We benefit from them all. Thankfully, most, do not have to make that choice nor would they want to.

Touch — I stroked the head of my son while he was falling asleep tonight. Such comfort can flow from hands. May your hands make what you touch come alive.

Smell — Have you enjoyed the fresh smell of rain, a pine forest, or the rich wonders of a rose? The gift of smell is all around you, calling you to enjoy with this sense.

Taste — In the springtime, everything seems just a little more alive. Taste in the physical sense, the bounty of the earth, and may you taste the sweetness of life, even finding after the bitterness, there is something good in it.

See — The wonder of sight in your days is incalculable. The images run and reflect where you have been, what you have done, and what brings you pleasure. May your eyes never forget what you have seen and may the days show you more wonder to behold!

Hear — A rushing river, a breathing child at rest, or the sound of a favorite song; all speak that we might listen. Listening is for learners and those who stop "the train" long enough to find their dreams. Too much noise never says very much any way. May you hear the voice that calls you into higher living.

# Exit and Arrival

The story is over but the journey continues, your new opportunities to finish well are only beginning. Every day and, really, every moment is breathless with anticipation. Finishing well is more about who you are and how you live then a place, status, or a position. I could have the whole world but be missing the best of it.

This was my cry, "I want to finish well." I am learning. Learning and being aware are always good companions in the race of life. Thank you to those I have been in the race with, I treasure you. To you, my reader, I hope you find something in these pages, just as a seeker would find gold. I am so pulling for you to finish well and I am so thankful I get to run with you on the race to the finish line.

Always the best, here and yet to come.

*Finish Well*

# Ideas That Travel Well as You Finish Well

– Take care of your body, soul, and mind. They are the places you put and bring life to.

– Take care of those you are connected with in life. If you can, find daily ways to make their day.

– Be organized, at least to the degree that makes your life simpler. Know where you put essential items, so you can grab and go! Less time and energy spent on non-essential issues means more time for happiness and less stress.

– Give yourself to pleasure. Engage all of you in what you enjoy and be glad you do.

– Make choices from your heart, not only your head. These choices always come back to talk to you later when you don't chose from the heart.

– Practice having a spirit of forgiveness for others and especially for yourself.

– Learn to value and enjoy people's differences and successes. You might just learn something or love someone. Jealousy tells you, you don't believe in your own worth. That is so far from the truth.

– Give yourself and others time, when at a difficult station in the race of life. Make time a friend, give a friend time.

– Remember where all blessings come from and that being thankful really does have heart and mind benefits.

– Don't leave this planet without love, giving and receiving love. I can think of no virtue so desirable as love and no place better to live in.

– Admit failure, a mistake, a sin, and error. It is too much of a burden to try to appear perfect. Imperfect people make the best lovers anyway.

– Take a trip outside of your comfort and sights. Change and many broken routines are good for everyone.

– Stand up when it is right and necessary. Sit down when it doesn't matter. Love covers the situation better than confrontation or hate.

– Always hope and never give up. Your new joys may be just around the corner.

– Every day do something for someone who can't thank you or won't.

– Appreciate who you are and are becoming. Write your own beautiful story and finish well.

# All I Have Learned...

Well, not all I have learned, or this would be a novel, but it is a compilation of life's good gifts and lessons learned. I am sure you have your good gifts and lessons. I hope these add to your delight. I hope you smile...and dance.

Never miss an opportunity
- to do good
- to say a kind word
- to listen to your desires (for they will come calling and ask of you)

See a sunset or sunrise...often. Watch it as though it was the first time you ever saw it.

As far as you can, make it right. When you cannot make it right, rest.

Always reserve the right to learn from your mistakes. Forgive yourself.

## Finish Well

Visit those who cannot visit you.

Don't let anyone change you. We are here to add to one another's lives, not take from them.

Be weak sometimes so someone can be useful to lift you up. Life is not only for the strong.

Tell your parents thank you for all they did for you, even if you are unhappy with some of their choices. Forgive others.

Surprise and tell someone in your past how their life has influenced yours through the years.

Go to sleep when overwhelmed, tired, or distressed. Magic happens through a good nap or purposed rest.

Take care of yourself. It is a way to tell yourself you are loved.

Kiss regularly. Mean it.

Travel...your view of the world will change and you will change.

Have children, if possible (search your heart to be sure if you don't). They open places your soul has never been.

Never lose passion. It is the fire that lights all activity with the flame that brightens living.

Go to college to develop yourself and your gifts. The world is waiting for the real you and nobody else can fill your spot!

Pet a contented animal and ask yourself if you have rest like they do.

Eat in joy, eat in health, eat in good conversation.

Appreciate small tokens of kindness and love. Value these and the one who gives you large ones.

Always make room for one more friend in your life.

Never hate. It only kills you.

*Finish Well*

# About the Cover

One of my favorite things is looking up. I cannot resist the heavens. From the breaking sun over the mountains or rising from the water (thank you, Hawaii), the heavens are filled with God's glory. I hunt for sunsets. As the day winds down, I look for skies to photograph. This evening shot was taken after a stormy Arizona winter day. Arizona hosts many cloudless days, but clouds add to and make beautiful sunsets. As I hiked to a high point in the desert, I caught this shot; it was my last photo after taking many pictures! At the time, I did not realize it would be the cover for *Finish Well*. It was a photograph of cheer and beauty for me as I saw the outstretched rays of the sun on the horizon. It was fitting to me, as sunsets close the day, signifying that the day finished well.

*Finish Well*